FROM THESE COMES MUSIC

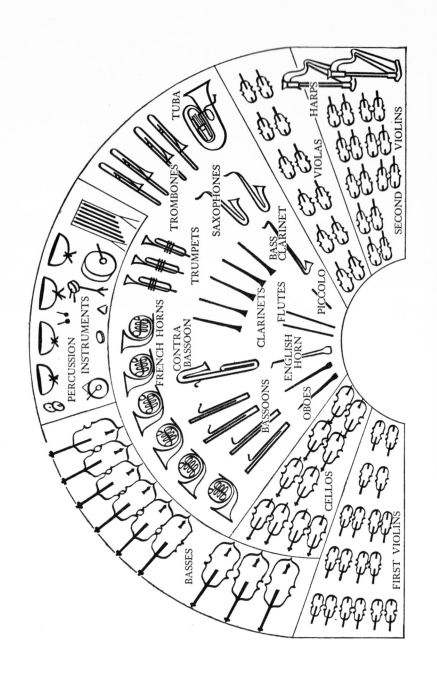

≫ HOPE STODDARD ≪

# FROM THESE
# COMES MUSIC

*Instruments of the Band and Orchestra*

ILLUSTRATED BY
AVA MORGAN

NEW YORK ≫ *Thomas Y. Crowell Company*

## BY THE AUTHOR

FROM THESE COMES MUSIC

SYMPHONY CONDUCTORS OF THE U.S.A.

*65104*

# ACKNOWLEDGMENTS

THE preparation for the writing of this book involved a special kind of research: I had discussions with at least one player on each instrument—one who had spent his life with it, who loved it, who had gone to great pains to perfect himself on it, who had built a useful and successful career around it. I also took a few lessons on the instrument, enough to get the feel of it under my fingers. Most important of all, I learned how to regard the instrument as its player does.

I wish to express my very real gratitude to these instrumentalists. I cannot begin to enumerate the instances of kindness, the inconveniences undergone by them, that I might be better informed. Without their wholehearted assistance, the book would not have been possible:

Violin ................Michael Rosenker, *Concert Master, New York Philharmonic Symphony Stadium concerts*

Viola ................Milton Katims, *National Broadcasting Company Symphony*

Violoncello........Samuel Mayes, *Boston Symphony* Leonard Rose, *New York Philharmonic Symphony*

Double Bass........Roger M. Scott, *Philadelphia Orchestra*
Philip Sklar, *National Broadcasting Company Symphony*

Harp ................Virginia Morgan, *San Francisco Symphony*
Edward Vito, *National Broadcasting Company Symphony*

Guitar ...............Vladimir Bobri, *Editor*, The Guitar Review *and President of the Society of the Classic Guitar of New York*
Andrés Segovia, *guitar virtuoso*

Transposition ....Sigurd Rascher, *concert saxophonist*

Tuba .................William Bell, *New York Philharmonic Symphony*
Joseph J. Novotny, *National Broadcasting Company Symphony Orchestra*
Joseph Tarto, *Band of America*

French Horn ....Arthur Berv, *National Broadcasting Company Symphony Orchestra*
Frank Brouk, *Cleveland Orchestra*
James Chambers, *New York Philharmonic Symphony*
Mason Jones, *Philadelphia Orchestra*
James Stagliano, *Boston Symphony*

Trombone..........Gordon Pulis, *New York Philharmonic Symphony*
Roger Smith, *Metropolitan Opera Orchestra*

ACKNOWLEDGMENTS

Trumpet ............Isidor Blank, *Metropolitan Opera Orchestra*
Samuel G. Krauss, *Philadelphia Orchestra*

Bassoon ..............William Polisi, *New York Philharmonic Symphony*

Clarinet ..............Robert McGinnis, *New York Philharmonic Symphony*

Oboe and English Horn........William Arrowsmith, *Metropolitan Opera Orchestra*

Flute and Piccolo .........Ben Gaskins, *New York Philharmonic Symphony*
William Kincaid, *Philadelphia Orchestra*

Saxophone..........Alfred Gallodoro, *American Broadcasting Company Staff Orchestra*

Bagpipe ..............Neil Duddy, Patrick F. Meagher, *bagpipers*

Percussion Instruments....Saul Goodman, *New York Philharmonic Symphony*

Piano..................Grace Castagnetta, *concert pianist*

Pipe Organ ........Edouard Nies-Berger, *New York Philharmonic Symphony*

Accordion..........Sergei Matusewitch, *concert accordionist*
Charles Nunzio, *Director, Nunzio Accordion School, Newark, N. J.*

ACKNOWLEDGMENTS

Harpsichord ......Sylvia Marlowe, *concert harpsichordist*

Carillon..............Kamiel Lefévere, *carillonneur, Riverside Church, New York*

Much of the material in this book was first published in *The International Musician.* I wish to thank its editor and publisher, Leo Cluesmann, for his kind permission to use it.

HOPE STODDARD

# CONTENTS

CONTENTS

# PART III ⫸ *Percussion Instruments*

# PART IV ⫸ *Keyboard Instruments*

FROM THESE COMES MUSIC

*Part 1*

»» STRINGED INSTRUMENTS ««

FOREWORD

STRINGS are sounded in three ways. They are bowed, as
with the violin, viola, violoncello, or bass viol; they are
plucked, as with the guitar, harp, or harpsichord (the latter by remote control); or they are struck (again by remote control), as with the piano.

Given equal tension, the longer the string the deeper
its tone; and, given equal length, the looser the string, the
deeper its tone.

The resonance box gives substance to the sound.
Thus the shape of the violin determines the sort of sound
it gives, as does the shape of the guitar or the harp.

*Pizzicato* means "plucking the string"; *double-stopping*
means finger work on two strings at once; *position* means
one of the arbitrary points at which the left hand halts on
the finger board.

## CHAPTER I

»» *The Violin* ««

*The violin is virtuosic,*
*Is played by Gypsy, Croat and Cossack,*
*And those whose playing's astronomic*
*Can play in double stops, harmonic.*

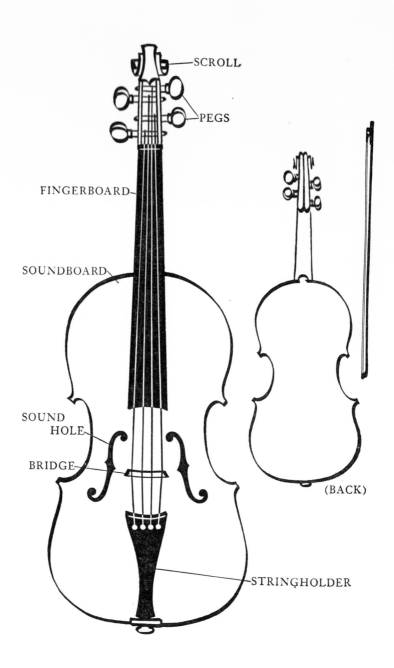

SCROLL

PEGS

FINGERBOARD

SOUNDBOARD

SOUND
HOLE

BRIDGE

STRINGHOLDER

(BACK)

# THE VIOLIN

SITTING across from Michael Rosenker, concert master of the New York Philharmonic-Symphony Stadium Series, I speculated on the violinist's three-sided existence.

As orchestra member he plays five nights a week. He rehearses twice a week and, of course, practices his parts at home. Unlike, say, the drummer, who has breathing spells between playing stints, he is required to be busy practically every minute during every composition. And he must play fresh programs each evening.

Then there is his busy teaching schedule, requiring far more than mere skill in imparting knowledge. Mr. Rosenker's face lighted up when he spoke of one particular pupil, a lad of seven, who already plays with masterly interpretation the Mendelssohn Concerto. One feels here is a projection of enthusiasm and purposefulness as well as knowledge.

Finally there is Rosenker's career as a virtuoso. He was to appear shortly as soloist at the Stadium in the taxing Dvořák Concerto. Then he was to appear in a concert of his own in Carnegie Hall, playing the new and difficult Violin Concerto by Nicolai Rakov in its first American performance, and the Duo Concertante by Stravinsky.

Among instrumentalists perhaps only the violinist becomes thus involved in a three-pronged career. What in the nature of the violin requires such versatility coupled with consecration?

It is partly, perhaps, because the violin is all but indispensable to our age. As the harp is the symbol of Ireland and the guitar of Spain, the violin might well be the symbol of the whole Western world. For it meets all the demands of our modern era, from both the aesthetic and the practical viewpoints. It is beautiful in tone. It can be carried almost as easily as a detective novel. Its upkeep offers no serious problem. It sounds well played either in groups or singly. It bulwarks the modern orchestra. It might almost be said to *make* the modern orchestra, since without it and the other strings the orchestra becomes a band. It gives an added touch to the modern dance ensemble. As a solo instrument it can rise singly and unaided above orchestra or chorus.

Its price is adjustable. The instrument sells at anything from $15 to $80,000. (The older it is the more it usually costs, since the better specimens improve with age.) Stradivarius made around 1116 violins in his lifetime, of which 540 or so are still in existence, each selling at between $10,000 and $80,000. Players' remunerations show as wide a range. Our great virtuosos realize concert fees in four digits. But street fiddlers play for a penny tossed in the hat.

"Fiddle," by the bye, is the authentic term, for all it has fallen into disrepute. It comes from "fiedel" (*fidula, vielle*), the medieval forerunner of our present-day instrument. The word "violin" derives from "viol," an instrument which bore but a superficial resemblance to our modern violin. This viol was flat of back. It had six strings and these were lighter and drawn less tightly than those of the violin, making loud playing difficult. Moreover the strings were tuned in fourths (except for one interval which was a third). Its neck was fitted with gut frets. The fiedel, on the other hand, was tuned in fifths (as is the violin), and was capable of sounding out loudly. Both of these instruments used a bow and hence both had that peculiarity in construction which makes bowing on several separate strings possible, the indented waistline. That early bow, however, was little other than the stringed half of the bow-and-arrow combination. In other words, it curved *out*.

François Tourte (1747-1835) practically invented the bow that violinists use today, which is 29⅛ inches long, bends inward toward the hair (horsetail strands), and is made tight or loose by a screwing gadget located in the part the hand grasps (the nut). The player loosens the hair in nonplaying intervals to ease tension on the bow. A violin bow has to be rehaired at anywhere from a month to a year, depending on how much it is used. To make it come to grips with the strings the player rosins it before playing. Rosin is that brittle amber-colored solid, used also in the manufacture of varnish, and formed as a residue in the distillation of oil of turpentine.

The conscientious violinist usually dusts the rosin from his instrument with a silk cloth after every session. Country fiddlers pride themselves on collecting a goodly crust of the stuff beneath the strings they so vigorously saw. They maintain that it improves the tone. What probably improves the tone is the amount of time it has taken them in practice to accrete that rosin.

The plain, good-quality bow costs around $75. One made by the famous bowmaker Tourte costs $1200.

The violin's four strings are tuned thus:

but this is no indication of its range, since the higher-position harmonics enable the violinist to go as high as the human ear can hear.

The strings are made either of wire or gut (cat or sheep gut is used) and are tightened by means of pegs inserted in the pegbox at the scroll end of the instrument (the neck). Strings have to be replaced at anywhere from a week to a year, depending on the usage. The bridge which holds the strings up from the instrument sometimes falls, and the sound post inside the instrument at rare intervals comes loose. Hence the "violin repair shops" tucked somewhere near every music center.

The fingering of the violin is good, straightforward stuff, namely to get the finger down firmly on exactly the right place, and hold it there while the note sounds. Because of certain principles having to do with vibrations, the fingers stop the strings (hold them down) at closer and closer intervals as they climb higher on the strings. (Note that frets on a guitar are placed closer together in the "high" regions.) The violinist must therefore negotiate intervals in the high positions with great finesse. Harmonics (made by placing the finger lightly on the string) require extra care, since they blur if the finger is even a whiff off position. Finesse also is required in the shifting of the left hand from position to position up the neck of the violin. Then there is the vibrato—that swelling and subsiding sound made by swaying the left-hand fingers on the strings. Moderately used, it is one of the most beautiful effects in string playing.

If manipulation of the left hand can accomplish accuracy of pitch and to some extent tonal beauty, it has mere pedestrian skill in comparison to the actions of the right hand and arm on the bow. Far from just getting that bow across the strings (to put them in vibration, of course) the player has to know how to hop and skip it, flick it and fling it, drag it and drawl it, lunge it and lilt it, swing it and ping it, spiccato and *saltando* and *martelé* and *détaché* and *sautillé* it. It has been said with some truth that the left hand is the artisan; the right, the artist.

Like all other stringed instruments, the violin can be muted by attaching a small gadget to the bridge. This muffles the tone, makes it somewhat gentler and more elusive. Violin strings are at times plucked. This pizzicato, done with the right-hand thumb or index finger, or more rarely with the left-hand fingers, produces a sharp, percussive effect not unlike the chirping of a cricket.

The violinist, like the instrument he plays, knows how to adjust to the modern music world's insistence on co-operative as well as solo effort. If he trains with one eye to a virtuoso career, the other is fixed as steadily on less spectacular but more predictable ways of earning a living.

This usually means orchestra membership and teaching. In both of these fields he must be absolutely dependable. Temperament is out. In the orchestra, be he second violin, first violin, or, among the latter, concert master, he must be able to concentrate with startling fixedness. He must notice every movement of the conductor, and his reactions must be almost telepathic.

The second violins of an orchestra rarely play in unison with the first violins, but rather an octave or other interval under them. Since they usually play on the lower strings, which do not respond so easily as the higher, they have tonal problems even surpassing the firsts in difficulty.

The concert master in the orchestra has special duties. He is a sort of second conductor, calling the orchestra to order at the beginning of a concert. Moreover, he is the mentor of his section, interpreting bowings and other markings. When *divisi* is called for—this is a splitting up of chords among the various desk men—the concert master decides how it is to be done. The other members in the first violin section take their bowings from him— thus the effect of uniform bowing in the orchestra. Moreover, the concert master often plays the solo part, all the other violins either remaining silent or filling in the harmony—as instance the following theme of Richard Strauss's *Ein Heldenleben:*

The concert master is the lone member of the string section playing along with the French horns in Brahms's

Symphony No. 1 in the following passage (second theme of the Second Movement):

To name all the outstanding passages for violin in our great symphonies, however, would be to list practically every composition in the repertoire, since the violin section shines at some point in every one. In short, the violin is employed to give sonority, sweetness, and stability to almost every group of chamber or orchestra caliber. Were it suddenly to pass out of existence, it would be necessary, if our Western conception of music were to survive, forthwith to reinvent it.

## CHAPTER II  -» *The Viola* «-

*Violas have a tempered sound,*
*They're quieting things to have around,*
*And even when they play their solos*
*They're still subdued like good violas.*

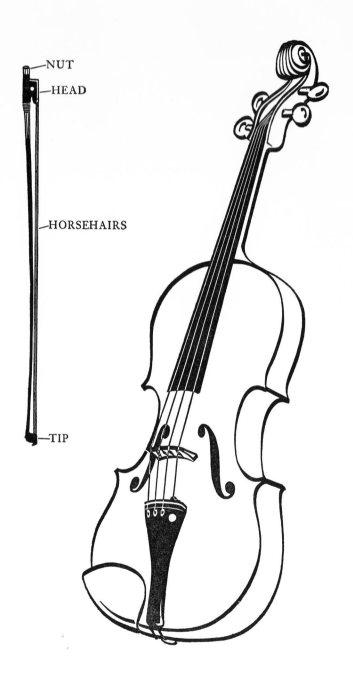

NUT

HEAD

HORSEHAIRS

TIP

# THE VIOLA

WHEN I started asking violists about their instrument, I expected the usual particularizations regarding tone, difficulties in playing, and place in the orchestra. In other words, just another instrument. I found out soon enough that the viola is more than that. It is a state of mind. Psychoanalysts, if they haven't done so already, should add the viola to their symbols, along with staircases, eggs, and snakes. For it is an instrument that is not merely played. It is lived in as in a country. Breathed like air. Imbibed like drink.

There are reasons for this. An instrument that only a highly complex civilization could have evolved, the viola implies other instruments: quartets, larger ensembles. It was fashioned to fit in groups. Its function is to provide support, to augment, to enrich, to clarify. With such a purpose, it was made just the right size for playing. If it had been given the size for fullest tone, it would have been gauged between the cello and the violin. But then the player would not have been able to hold it under his chin. Not so long ago just such a viola was fashioned. It was to be held like a cello (longer peg, of course) and bowed like one. But it looked strange, was hard to manage, was unpopular. Today violists stick to the under-the-chin position and violas range in size from fourteen to eighteen inches. Result: they sound a bit veiled, on the throaty side. But the tone, through its very limitations, gains in mellowness, in persuasiveness. And the viola remains outstandingly *useful*. This idea of service saturates its players.

Another reason for the instrument's tendency to enmesh its players in a special state of mind: the viola is by nature and circumstance submerged in the orchestral texture. In the eighteenth century violists just played along an octave above the double bass or oompahed while the violins played the principal part. They were the pale double of the basses and second violins. If the first violin couldn't play very well, he was demoted to second; if he didn't make the grade there, he was put in the viola section. Forsythe in his book on orchestration recalls "the bad old days when viola players were selected merely because they were too wicked or too senile to play the violin." True, there were exceptions. There are distinctive passages for viola in Bach's Brandenburg Concerto No. 6. Alessandro Rolla, Paganini's teacher, wrote a duet for viola and violin in which the violin plays second fiddle to the viola. (How violists chortle over that!) Karl Stamitz (1746-1801) wrote at least two concertos for it, probably for his tours of Europe as a virtuoso on the instrument. Berlioz in his *Harold in Italy* gave it serious recognition. Haydn and Mozart, moreover, through their thoughtful scoring, made it an integral and responsible member of the string quartet.

In spite of these happy exceptions, it must be recorded that by and large few seventeenth and eighteenth century composers knew how to write for the viola. Its part clung to the violin's, cello's, or double bass's. Or it was liaison agent between two sections. Beethoven rarely took the viola above the third position. (Intricate playing requires all of the seven-plus positions.) But he nevertheless had fun with it as he did with most of the knotty problems of his life. He wrote a duo for viola and cello "with eye-glass obbligato" since both players for whom it was written were bespectacled.

The tendency to belittle the viola carried over to the nineteenth century. Wagner scored passages for it in which the tremolo continues for what seems, to violists at least, eternities. Brahms, on the other hand, came out heartily in favor of the instrument. But then he was all but modern.

With the dawn of the twentieth century, with its encouragement of enterprise in the ranks, composers began to allow violas to move anywhere. They were no longer tied to violin, cello, or bass but could take top or bass of a chord. Their range was extended. Violists started to climb their finger boards with the agility of violinists. In short, the viola began to display a personality of its own.

Composers have achieved greater independence for the instrument largely by following (and may my puns be forgiven me!) the Primrose path. For it is William Primrose, a native of Scotland, who has paved the way toward fuller expressiveness on the instrument. (Maurice Vieux of France and Lionel Tertis of England preceded him in this good office.) Thus a whole series of composers—Bax, Scott, Bridge, Vaughan Williams, Walton, Bowen—have brought into being a repertoire for the viola worthy of its scope, one requiring of the player the same development of and finesse in technique as is asked of the violinist or cellist.

Richard Strauss, with exquisite discrimination, has the viola take the part of Sancho Panza while the cello portrays Don Quixote. Georges Enesco in his *Roumanian Rhapsody* shows good feeling for the viola. Hindemith (a violist himself) scores knowingly for it. Morton Gould, R. Russell Bennett, Milhaud, Bartók, and Tansman have written viola concertos. Today's violist in developing his repertoire has many fine concertos from which he may choose.

What is this curious instrument, so long subdued yet so necessary to the orchestra's texture? It is one fifth lower than the violin. In other words, you get its range by eliminating the upper string of the violin (both instruments are tuned in fifths) and stringing a thicker string a fifth lower than the violin's lowest string, G.

The viola uses the alto clef.

Requirements for playing the instrument are strong, large, flexible hands, a cooperative spirit, and a flair for basking in anonymity. Since the viola's strings are larger and thicker than the violin's, greater pressure is required of the left fingers as well as more concentrated pressure of the bow hand. In fact, the whole articulation has to be a bit firmer. Passages must be assayed distinctly and fluently rather than lightly and rapidly. The left hand must have the ability to stretch great distances, and the vibrato has to be wider and more intense. The bow of the viola is a bit shorter than that of the violin, making it more wieldy on the heavier strings.

Ten to twelve violas are usually the complement of major symphony orchestras, and their seating position is as a rule front center. Six are the requisite for smaller orchestras. One of the violists is the "solo" and plays the passages so designated. Aside from this leader in his section, there are no "firsts" or "seconds" as there are in the violins. All violas play the same music—with one exception. When the conductor orders *divisi*, the outside violists play the upper line and the inside the lower. Or, if the conductor wants the part divided three ways, the first pair of violists plays one part; the second pair, another; the third yet another. And so on down (or up) the line.

The special problems of violists in symphony orchestras are these: They have to be very careful to temper the sound not only in pitch but also in dynamics. For they often play the fifth above the prime, and this fifth can set a new tonality if it is the least bit exaggerated. If they are too loud or too insistent, another key is established. They can throw a whole string section out of kilter. Thus they have to deal in subtleties not required of the principals. They have another task: They must suggest at times which direction the development is taking, and so must underline or exaggerate where necessary.

Thus violists, who have it in their power to upset the whole social structure of the orchestra, yet who fulfill patiently year after year their task of filling in, must have not only the physical requirements of playing and a love for their instrument but a social consciousness above the ordinary. As one violist put it to me, "If the inhabitants of the world were only one-tenth as cooperative as the members of the viola section of a symphony orchestra, we'd *get* somewhere!"

But the violist is something besides all this. These grave watchers over symphonic weal are usually the intellectuals of the orchestra. Philosophic they must be to remain in their position. But they accentuate this tendency by shifting their gaze outside working hours to the horizons of science, politics, and art. They have libraries. They collect antiques. They play chess rather than poker. They have opinions. They discuss. They ponder.

Discerning concertgoers sense this when they hear the voice of the viola in a symphony or chamber music group. Or when they listen to an exquisite designation such as it is accorded in Debussy's Trio for Flute, Viola, and Harp. They note that the players, like their instruments, have mellowness, graciousness, dignity. They detect as well a natural sensitivity, such as one violist indicated when he told me with an aggrieved shrug: "At least proofreaders have got out of the habit of thinking 'violist' is just a misspelling of 'violinist' and of altering the word accordingly!"

CHAPTER III ⟫⟫ *The Violoncello* ⟪⟪

*The cello's tone is rich and broad,*
*It's fun to play but very hard.*
*Its literature goes on and on,*
*So do not overdo "The Swan."*

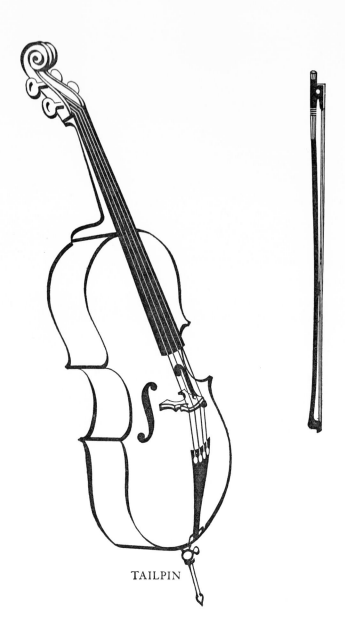

TAILPIN

# THE VIOLONCELLO

SUPPOSE you have spent weeks up in a balloon in the stratosphere surrounded by silence. Suppose, as you descend, you hear coming up from the earth's green surface a single tone—the murmur of a forest, the roar of the ocean, or perhaps just wind sighing across the plain. Suppose this sound spells to you your kinship with human-kind, your ties to earth, your love of all the good things of life. Then you will be having just the feeling the listener has on hearing, in the midst of Strauss's *Don Quixote* or Beethoven's Fifth, the violoncello's tone rising above the current of the orchestra.

But this sound is not the carefree expression of bird or wind. The violoncello might be pictured on the facade of any public building as a symbol of human pertinacity. For with perhaps no other invention, certainly no other musical instrument, has man's ingenuity so widened scope, so extended horizons. The heavy strings might tempt toward plodding fingers; the relatively short bow to chopped phrasing; the long fingerboard to jagged jumps and faulty intonation. Yet in the hands of an expert the cello is neither pedestrian, uneven nor hampered. Its *crescendos* and *decrescendos* do not cover changes in bow arm but accord with music's long line. Its phrases come out clean, with no least nod toward string crossings. Its scale is equal-

ized from the lowest note to the highest with no conces-
sion to positions or fingerings. Its slides have been made
inaudible through the finger extension system of Pablo
Casals. Through the ceaseless struggles of players who
have held musicianship above virtuosity and perfection
above ease, the cello has graduated from being the floor
of the quartet to being a purveyor of deep and poignant
emotion.

The cello (this word is used in place of "violoncello"
much as "piano" is used in place of "pianoforte") encompasses in its four strings over three and a half octaves:

The different notes are obtained—as they are on all stringed
instruments—by shortening or lengthening the vibrating
portion of the string. The cellist sets the string in motion
by passing his bow over it, while one of his left-hand
fingers or his thumb presses down that string, cutting off
a portion from vibration. Cello fingering (unlike violin
fingering) is by semitones, only the first and second fingers
on occasion being allowed to stretch a whole tone. As the
hand goes above the fourth position the thumb forms on
the two lower strings a sort of movable fret beyond which
the other fingers may operate. Here, because of the
shorter distances between intervals, the fingering approximates more closely that of the violin.

Because of the length of the fingerboard and the thick-
ness of the strings, and also because of the position of the

cello neck and the fingering hand, the cellist resorts to probably a greater variety of left finger pressures and positions than any other instrumentalist. In fact, he varies the pressure of his index finger as need dictates from direct contact at the extreme tip to pressure from the side almost as far down as the first joint.

Because cello strings vary greatly in level, and because the arc the cellist describes in sounding all four strings is much wider than that of the violin or viola, bowing requires agility of a superlative sort. String skips, double-stopping and arpeggios deftly executed become the study of a lifetime.

An item regarding one of the cello's accessories: The adoption some fifty years ago of the tail-pin, that contrivance which lifts the cello from the floor by about a foot, has had the curious result of putting the instrument within women's professional scope. Today one or two women, sometimes more, are to be found in most of the cello sections (made up, all told, of about ten players) of our major symphony orchestras. Raya Garbousova has carved a sure niche for herself on the concert stage, as did before her Beatrice Harrison and Guilhermina Suggia.

Of the male contingency, one must count among great cellists, besides the incomparable Pablo Casals, Gregor Piatigorsky, who regularly tours this continent, the late Emanuel Feuermann, and that teacher who was instructor to practically all the leading American cellists of today, the late Felix Salmond.

It is difficult to say whether the quartet brought out the cello or the cello brought out the quartet. Perhaps it was a two-way affair. At any rate, the cello emerged later than the violin as an ensemble instrument. Its tardiness was due no doubt to the competition exerted by the viola da gamba, the standard chamber and orchestral bass of the seventeenth century. The larger and more thickly strung cello was used at first only to strengthen the bass section of church choirs.

The viola da gamba, however, when it was first used to accompany the violin's thrilling tones (pianos were yet to be invented) proved such frail support that the violoncello, with its greater volume, began to supplant it. For the same reason the cello became indispensable to the string quartet. Haydn and Boccherini, not content with having it provide underpinning, began to depend on it for solo effects. Haydn's early quartets had the cello just filling in; his later ones had all four instruments playing in perfect balance.

Mozart, with his knack for mingling and merging instrumental voices, carried the good work further. There was a personal reason for his solicitude. Frederick William, King of Prussia, was a competent cellist. He was also Mozart's patron. He desired—and deserved, such were his attainments—richer cello parts than the chamber music of that day afforded. Mozart saw that he got them. He wrote quartets in which themes were about equally divided between violin and cello. He even gave the cello solo prominence, as in the D Major Quartet's Minuet. With this advance, figurations and passage work entailing rapid scales and string crossings became a "must" for cellists.

Beethoven realized the instrument's full possibilities in

polyphonic playing. Then came the massed tonal effects of Schubert, Schumann, Mendelssohn, and Brahms—until the quartet became as expressive within its scope as is the symphony orchestra within its.

Composers have not overlooked the cello's possibilities in other fields, either. Handel gave to the cello the obbligato parts to "O Liberty" (*Judas*), "What passion cannot music raise" (*St. Cecelia's Day*) and "But O sad Virgin" (*L'Allegro*). Bach wrote for it six suites so far in advance of their time that they have only recently been brought into the cellist's regular repertoire. This was due largely to the good services of Casals. His discovery of them while rummaging in a secondhand shop took place while he was still very young. As he writes, "My attention was suddenly arrested by some unaccompanied suites of Bach for cello. I forgot entirely the reason for my visit to the shop and could only stare at this music which nobody had told me about. Sometimes even now, when I look at the covers of that old music, I see again the interior of that old and musty shop with its faint smell of the sea. I took the suites home and read and reread them. For twelve years after that I studied and worked every day at them. I was nearly twenty-five before I had the courage to play one of them in public."

Finding these manuscripts of Bach has been but one of many of Casals' services to cellists—to all music lovers. He organized a symphony orchestra in Barcelona, Spain; through his concertizing here and abroad he has brought a new conception of sensitive cello playing as well as orchestral conducting to the whole world; during the past several summers he has directed music festivals in Prades, France, specializing in works of Bach.

Incidentally, even Bach's cello suites were not all of them written for the cello as we know it but for a five-stringed affair which Bach himself invented (an E-string added at the top of the register) and which has since gone out of use.

Haydn, generous with the cello in all his works, scored solo passages for it in six of his symphonies.

In the Romantic period, Rossini in the Overture to *William Tell,* introduced a quintet for five solo cellos. These were accompanied pizzicato by the other cellos.

Beethoven utilized the dignified, grave tone of the cellos playing in unison in his Fifth Symphony:

Modern composers—Hindemith, Prokofiev, Khachaturian, Bloch ("Schelomo"), Milhaud, Barber, Shulman, Villa-Lobos (his *Bachianas Brasileiras* is scored for eight cellos, no other instruments participating)—make no concessions whatever to cellists, score for extreme ranges, use wide jumps both of finger and bow, concoct weird progressions. But in some cases earlier composers were just as rigorous. The solo in Beethoven's Triple Concerto (violin, cello, piano) is as hard as anything written since, and the solo in Haydn's Post-Horn Symphony is nothing to sniff at, either. Perhaps the most famous cello solo (barring the ubiquitous "Swan" of Saint-Saëns) is that in the third movement of Brahms' Piano Concerto:

It brings out all the deep, rich tones of the instrument.

In citing compositions which have enriched the cellist's repertoire, one's thoughts turn again inevitably to Casals. He repopularized the cello sonatas of Beethoven and of Brahms, as well as concertos of Haydn, Schumann, Lalo, and Dvořák. He played them, in fact, when box-office receipts indicated the desirability of a different sort of musical fare. He played them so often that at last audiences grew to love them and call for them.

Of such stuff as this are pioneers made!

## CHAPTER IV

->>> *The Double Bass* <<<-

*The double bass which plays quite loud*
*Should not be carried in a crowd;*
*It bows and thumps and pizzicatos,*
*And does not fit in tiny grottoes.*

WORM GEAR

# THE DOUBLE BASS

CALL it double bass, contrabass, bass viol, bull fiddle, dog-house, or just plain bass, that sleek, space-consuming tone-maker of the viol family lined in sixes to tens across the back or down the side of our symphony orchestras un-doubtedly bulwarks the whole ensemble in an aural as well as a visual sense. It's loud. It's deep. It's time-setting. It's percussive.

Composers only of late have come to rely on it in all these aspects. Back in the days of Jean Baptiste Lully (1632-1687) when the double bass was used primarily to imitate storms and tempests, it was not a "regular" in sym-phony orchestras. Perhaps the lack of its time-setting bow stroke and its metronomic string twang was one of the reasons Lully had to direct the orchestra by thumping a heavy staff on the floor. Perhaps even his death was at-tributable to the absence of double basses, because his cud-gel once missed the floor and landed on his foot. An abscess developed. Blood poisoning set in. He was gath-ered unto his fathers. And the moral of this is: always have double basses in orchestras to help set the beat.

In 1757 the double bass became a steady in the Paris Orchestra, but they had only one, and its performance was reserved for Fridays, the day of great spectacles. This at least gave the instrument a toe hold in the orchestra. From then on people got used to the basses' rhythmic pulsation. Beethoven, among his other contributions to good scoring, apportioned such notes to the bass as made it "set" the phrases played by the other instruments. In the finale of his Ninth Symphony

the bass by its added burst of sound gets across that sense of triumphant jubilation required. Then it was Beethoven who brought the double bass first into orchestral prominence, when in the Third Movement (third theme) of his Fifth Symphony he has it doubling with the cellos in this highly rhythmical melody:

He wrote this, it is said, with an eye to that great virtuoso who practically revolutionized double-bass playing, Domenico Dragonetti. The bassists from Beethoven's time on considered themselves responsible for the loudness or softness, length or shortness, pointedness or blandness of the over-all orchestral tone.

Wagner gave the bass even more rein. He began to write independent lines for it—make it say something in its own right. Certain passages in his works—for instance, the introduction to *Die Walküre*—are used in Metropolitan Opera Orchestra auditions as a test of bassists' all-around ability: their technical facility, the color and luster of their tones, their interpretative gifts. Mahler gave the bass a chance to show its melodic possibilities when he scored a great sweeping passage for it in the Third Movement of his First Symphony:

Composers old and new have been like putty when confronted with the temptation to use the bass for "effects." Beethoven cast it as thunder in the storm scene of his *Pastoral*, and made it imitate the dull sound of the rolling stone in the famous grave-digging scene in *Fidelio*. Respighi employed it for the lion's roar in *Feste Romane*. Saint-Saëns had it suggest the elephant's dance in his *Carnival of the Animals*. And Prokofiev made it a laugh-provoker in his *Lieutenant Kije*.

But it is in the swing bands that the double bass is exploited in every inch of its six-foot height. There's pizzicato, for instance—so often used as to make bowing sound like a novelty. Not that symphonic orchestras don't go in for string-plucking, too. In symphonies, pizzicato is punctuation. The double bass provides the commas and dashes and periods of the orchestral conversation. When, for instance, the bassoon holds sustained notes, the double bass pizzicato gives each long note a little accent, a little push. In jazz orchestras, however, pizzicato is vocabulary as well as punctuation. In its special swing version the double bass is accompanied by a "slap" of the instrument—the dry crack obtained by twitching the strings extra hard so that they rebound against the finger board.

The niche for the double bass is carved still deeper in jazz orchestras by the instrument's knack of breaking rhythms, of employing profusely double notes and notes in the extreme upper and lower registers. Jazz bassists complement the left-hand work of the piano—no lazy man's job. Besides, they thump on the wood, get a guitar effect by plucking the strings with the fingernail, and twang above as well as below the bridge. The double bass is now as much in demand in the jazz orchestra as the trumpet, saxophone, and drums.

Bass players have conquered yet another field. They are soloists—both with symphony orchestras and in one-man recitals. For this work the bass is tuned a tone higher, and the bridge is made a shade lower, this to render the tone more brilliant. Serge Koussevitzky toured as bass soloist before he was a conductor, and it is perhaps due to this that the bass section of the Boston Symphony Orchestra became such a marvel of precision. A concert of the Philadelphia Orchestra once featured Anton Torello —principal bass player with that orchestra for thirty-four years and teacher of bassists now scattered all over the country in most of our major symphony orchestras—in the Concerto in A by Dragonetti. Wrote music critic Howard Taubman at that time: "Mr. Torello skipped along in rapid passages with dazzling dispatch and sang the broad passages of the slow movement with sustained line. There are many high notes in the concerto, and Mr. Torello had to stretch down near the bridge. At such moments he looked like a wrestler at affectionate grips with a fond, familiar opponent."

"Wrestler" is the word. The bassist battles a string five or six times as thick and as long as a violin's. Pressure of his bow as well as pressure of his fingers must be greater than that on lighter stringed instruments. He slides through seven positions besides the "thumb" positions, sounding the following note range on the four strings E, A, D, and G:

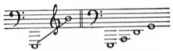

Note that the double bass is a transposing instrument—the only one in the string family. Thus, its *written* music is an octave higher than the foregoing example.

The upper positions require the bassist to slip the thumb from behind the neck and use it as a guide in placing his fingers in position. These thumb positions were especially favored by Richard Strauss. Double-stopping is another familiar device of bassists. The strings to be stopped are usually pulled nearer each other by fingers otherwise not in use, to make the stopping less sprawly. Of all the hazards of double-bass playing, however, the lengthy passage without rest is the worst. Composers are not expected to be indulgent of instrumentalists, but we wonder if Brahms knew what discomfort he was causing when he asked for a continuous *fortissimo* C from the double bass for eight or nine consecutive bars in his First Symphony. And surely Tchaikovsky evinced a certain callousness when in his Sixth Symphony he had the double bass play, again fortissimo, twenty-nine bars of low F-sharp tremolo.

Partly offsetting the numerous difficulties of the instrument is the fact that the length of the string (forty-three inches) makes harmonics sound better than on violin, viola, or even cello. It follows that harmonics are frequently used. They increase the instrument's range vastly, getting it well up into the violin register.

Credit for making the double bass adequate, orchestrally speaking, must go to inventors as well as to ardent instrumentalists. There's the contra C attachment, for instance —the means by which the length of the lowest string is increased by 6¾ inches, opening for the double bass— and for the whole orchestra, in fact—the vista of four extra semitones. Thus the range of the double bass is extended down to:

This attachment, reaching along the pegbox and above the scroll, works like this: four keys lie conveniently under the fingers in the first position. The first key (nearest the scroll) locks in E, the next in E-flat, the third in D, and the fourth in D-flat. With no key pressed at all, the string sounds C. Stravinsky, always quick to sense new orchestral possibilities, used the extra semitones for the opening of the *Firebird Suite*, and many passages in Wagner and Richard Strauss also require it.

This small gadget has in many cases proved an effective substitute for the five-string bass.

Another contrivance which has lessened headaches for the bassist is the "worm gear," a small wheel edged with teeth. This, fitted on the pegbox, so holds the string that one can tune it with hairbreadth precision and with no more force than it takes to wind a watch. Moreover, there is no danger of the string's slipping.

Whenever instruments offer particularly formidable technique, it is inevitable that different "schools" are developed. So bassists are sharply differentiated according to whether they use the German or the French method of bowing. The German way—fingers placed *under* the frog with the thumb above—was the earlier method. The French way—the fingers placed *over* the frog, the thumb holding from under the stick—was developed when the French stick was developed, around the turn of the nineteenth century. This stick is about twenty-five inches long, two inches shorter than the German one. The latter, however, has a wider frog.

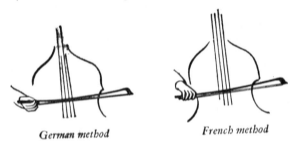

German method        French method

Pizzicato is essayed differently in the two schools. In the German school the little finger loops through the frog while the bow swings downward. In the French way the bow is held upward toward the scroll, much as in cello and violin playing, with the free finger plucking the string.

The complexities of technique are by no means the only difficulty the double bass player encounters. His whole professional life is a struggle to lick the transportation problem. "You can't carry a bass in a hard case," resignedly explains Philip Sklar of the N.B.C. Symphony Orchestra, "and the soft waterproof case just doesn't give adequate protection. Every time I get into a cab something happens. Just today the edge of a door hit my bridge and slid it over to one side! Going through a swinging door, your hands are full; you're helpless. And what do folks do? They just let the door swing! I have to back away quickly. And then the elevators!" Here he pauses, rolls his eyes up, and is eloquently silent.

What manner of men are these who choose—who *choose*—to spend a goodly portion of their lives sweating out background music, who trudge along with these overgrown papooses cluttering up their encounters with swinging doors, bus steps, and taxis; who only once in a blue moon attain to solo prominence and are otherwise content to be the blur behind the arpeggio, the rumble behind the theme song? Whatever they have in common, it is certainly not a yen for keeping in the spotlight. They choose the bass because it opens up a novel approach to music, allows for inventiveness, implies the earnest life, offers professional security. They choose it because they want an adversary worthy of serious struggle, because double basses are indispensable in the orchestra, because they like the sound of the thing. We half believe the latter reason carries more weight than any of the others. There's the story of the double bass player who had played ten years in an opera orchestra, his back to the stage. Then one evening he decided to view the performance from the

auditorium. "You know what?" he excitedly told a sec-
tionmate afterward. "When we are playing that beautiful
oompah, oompah part of ours in *Carmen*, there's a fellow
up there on the stage who cuts right in and sings along
with us:

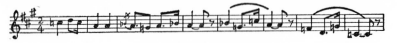

CHAPTER V  »»*The Harp* ««

*The harp's for angels, so they say,*
*And yet it's devilish hard to play!*

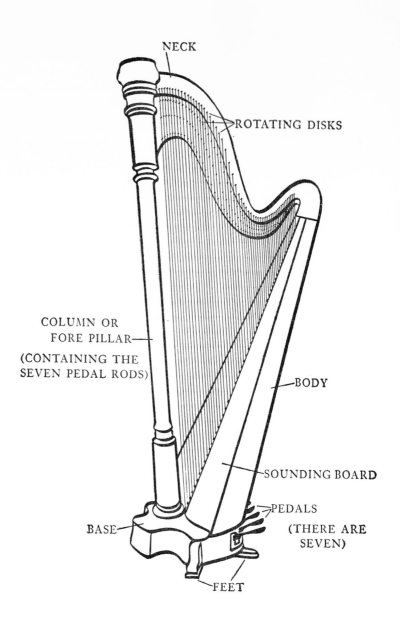

NECK

ROTATING DISKS

COLUMN OR
FORE PILLAR—

(CONTAINING THE
SEVEN PEDAL RODS)

BODY

SOUNDING BOARD

PEDALS

(THERE ARE
SEVEN)

BASE—

FEET

# THE HARP

THE harp is an instrument of paradoxes. It is called the oldest instrument in existence. Yet its present form came into being as late as 1811. It is an instrument studied more by women than by men. Yet—if one thinks of transportation problems alone—it is scarcely an instrument of feminine proportions. One is supposed to look like an angel playing it. Yet if one is to play it properly one must work like the—well, very hard indeed.

Beautiful the instrument certainly is, both in the music it transmits and in the form it takes. It would be hard to conceive of a structure more fully realizing beauty through practicability. The sounding board (the side resting against the player) grows broader and fuller toward the base not only for greater resonance but also to allow for the pedal mechanism in the pedestal. The column (the side perpendicular to the floor when the instrument is resting) is pillarlike instead of spikelike, so that its hollow center may accommodate the rods connecting the pedal mechanism with the strings. The neck (the curved bracket at the top) is broad to allow space for the mechanism changing the pitch. The neck is down-curved as it nears the player's side because, high notes requiring but short strings, less space is needed here for holding the strings. That graceful, triangular form, then, is no artist's flight of fancy.

It is as truly a product of need as are a bird's wings. For it makes possible the instrument's wide range—its full quota of notes.

That the harp is short on notes is a criticism that even its bitterest enemy could not level against it. The harp has more notes—meaning ways of sounding the various musical designations—than even the piano. For the harp has separate devices for playing enharmonic equivalents such as B-flat and A-sharp, or F, and E-sharp. In fact, the harp is the only instrument among those of fixed tones (such as piano, harpsichord, pipe organ, carillon, xylophone, marimba) which has a separate note for each sharp, flat, and natural. It thus in its very construction parallels written music more closely than does any other instrument.

There are only forty-seven strings on the harp, that is, six and a half octaves corresponding in scale to the white notes of the piano, with a range:

This in itself would be a rather limited outlay of notes. But the pedals serve to triple the number. Each of the seven pedals flaring out from the base (called the pedestal) controls one note in the octave. That is, one pedal controls *all* the C strings on the harp, another pedal controls *all* the D strings, another *all* the E strings, and so on through the scale. When any one pedal is raised, its note—say it is G —becomes flatted in *all* its octaves. When the pedal is lowered, all those G notes become sharped. When the pedal stays in the middle, all the notes stay natural.

The pedal action, once it has been transferred by means of the rods running up inside the column, manipulates the strings according to the accompanying diagram:

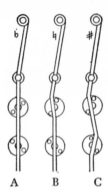

In A the string is shown at its longest and therefore its lowest. This is the "flat" position. Then in B the upper disk has turned, shortening the string and thereby raising it in pitch by a semitone. It is now in the "natural" position. In C the lower disk has turned, shortening the string still another semitone and putting it in the "sharp" position. As we said, forty-seven strings—seven to the octave—in various colors to assist the eye, lie under the harpist's fingers. If he puts all the pedals (they can be held in place through a notching device) in the raised position, forty-four of the strings (the highest and the two lowest strings have no pedal attachment) become flatted. If he puts all the pedals into the lower notch, the forty-four strings become sharped. It is evident that on the harp, transposition—quick change from one key to another—is all a matter of mastering the pedaling. In other words, a harp player may repeat a passage in another key *using exactly the same fingering.* Scale fingering, that bugbear of the pianist, is therefore to the harpist scarcely a problem at all. Incidentally, the harpist uses only four fingers on each hand. The little finger is out of alignment and is not used.

This instrument, adequate by all symphonic standards, was a product of the ingenuity of the piano maker, Sébastien Érard, who in 1810 perfected the double-action principle. Previous to that the harp,* with an incomplete scale, was hampered by the harpist's having to tune individual notes as he went along, in order to approximate sharps and flats. Not that the harpist hasn't still special problems of his own. So "set" are the harp's scales that some extra thinking is required when it comes to modulation. In radio work especially, where the harp is rapidly carving a sizeable niche for itself through its ability to create "atmosphere," fill in during interludes, provide a background for dialogue, the ability to make quick mental adjustments and sense enharmonic equivalents is all but indispensable. So when, instead of allowing a blank spot, the radio station employs a harpist to fill in the period, it is careful to employ one who can improvise in any split-second timing required. The enharmonic-minded harpist, who thinks in sounds rather than in notes, can go on indefinitely, changing keys or adjusting himself in any way to the program.

* The modern harp bears little relationship to the Celtic harp. That early harp is the one musical instrument that has been adopted as a national symbol (Eire's). In Wales, at one time, it was the only personal possession that could not be confiscated for debt. Every noble house in Wales was as sure to have its own hereditary harp as its coat of arms—a harp handed down through the centuries for the use of the household's bard.

In symphony orchestras, where the programs are re-hearsed and fairly stable, where beauty of tone and tech-nical facility are the requisites, women harpists have their innings. In fact, this is the one section of our symphony orchestras in which the women far outnumber the men. Audiences' sense of the rightness of this arrangement rests not on custom, for the practice itself is fairly new. When in 1930 Edna Phillips was appointed by Leopold Stokow-ski as harpist of the Philadelphia Orchestra, she was the only woman to hold a first harpist position with a major symphony orchestra. The sense of fitness rests rather on the finesse of women's playing and on the manner in which beauty of line in player supplements beauty of line in in-strument, on the delicate tilt of head, on the delicate play of hands.

Speaking of hands, though, let us be fair to the men, too. One of the most moving exhibits at the Chicago Art Insti-tute, "Study of Hands," is the painting of the hands, held in harp position, of Edward Vito, first harpist of the Na-tional Broadcasting Company Symphony Orchestra. Harpist Carlos Salzedo considers the movements of the hands on the strings a sort of dance and teaches his pupils so to consider them. Such an approach points to wide use of the harp in television.

Mr. Salzedo has proved himself in other ways mentor and innovator. He created the Salzedo Harp Ensemble, consisting of seven harps, which, during its various tours of the country, served to widen knowledge of the harp and harp music. He organized harp festivals in various centers of the United States. At his suggestion the Polish artist

Witold Gordon designed the "Salzedo Model" harp, used by many leading harpists. He conducts a Summer Harp Colony in Camden, Maine, where a good percentage of our nation's harpists are taught. He has composed works for the harp and has had works composed for his use—for instance, the Triple Concerto for Harp, Flute, Cello, and Orchestra by Bernard Wagenaar.

As a chamber music instrument, the harp figures in harp-flute-cello, in harp-flute-violin-viola-cello, in harp-violin-piano and other combinations. Salzedo has composed a Concerto for Harp and Seven Wind Instruments.

One harp at least is a requisite of every full symphony orchestra, with two or more employed in the major orchestras. Not that the harp is played in every composition or even in every program. For long stretches the harpist may sit silent, may not appear on the stage at all during the course of some programs. But then, suddenly, he will be called on to play a solo which gives tone to the whole concert. The caviar of the orchestra, in short.

The problem of tuning is especially acute in orchestral work, this because atmospheric conditions affect not only the harp but the wind instruments as well. For instance, when the harpist plays a passage with the flutist—say, Debussy's "Nuages"—he must compare carefully the pitches of the two instruments and temper his own to the flute's. Liszt's *Les Préludes* has a passage for harp and French horn that is "exposed," to use orchestral vernacular. Now the harp luckily has a series of harmonics here for the left hand alone. So, while this hand negotiates these harmonics, the right hand reaches up to the neck of the instrument and tunes (by means of a key) each individual note as the playing progresses. A similar procedure is necessary in Richard Strauss's tone poem, *Death and Transfiguration*. At the beginning the harp plays with the solo violin, later with the solo flute. By the time the finale of the *Transfiguration* is reached, the winds have warmed up and consequently gone up in pitch. Thus here again the harp has to tune note by note as it goes along.

Perhaps Debussy of all composers scores for harp with the deftest touch. Think of his *La Mer*, of his *Prelude à l'Après-midi d'un faune*, his *Danse sacrée*:

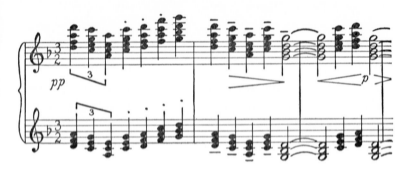

and you will hear the harp more pronouncedly than any other instrument. In fact, it is impossible to think of Debussy's music without sensing the harp's drifting arpeggios. His *Danse sacrée* and *Danse profane* were originally composed for *chromatic* harp, an instrument constructed one string for each tone, with practically no mechanism. Ravel, another Frenchman—members of this nationality seem to have a special affinity for the harp—gives evidence of the mastery of the sustained solo-and-arpeggio combination in his Introduction and Allegro septet:

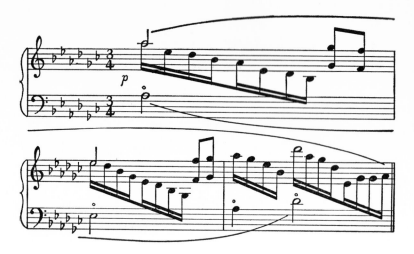

Saint-Saëns has composed an effective Fantasia for Violin and Harp.

Italian composers have good harp sense, too. Puccini knew how to utilize harp effects to good purpose, as did Rossini and Verdi. Sodero has realized good harpistic effects in the chords played arpeggio of his *Fantasia drammatica.* Malipiero's *Sonata à Cinque,* for harp, flute, violin, viola, and cello, which had its first performance in 1925, is also a worthy addition to the harpist's repertoire.

German composers do not come off so well. Wagner, though he was one of the first composers to give the harp a prominent place—at Bayreuth the harp parts were often quadrupled—often exploited it, in flourishes and such, in unharpistic effects.

Moreover, his harp passages sometimes call for a technique verging on the impossible, as in the "Fire Music" passage from *Die Walküre:*

However, we forgive him everything when we hear, in the Finale of *Das Rheingold*, the six harps each performing an independent scheme of arpeggios to provide heavenly music for the gods entering Valhalla. Arturo Toscanini, when he conducts this work, insists on keeping to the original and sometimes has six or seven harps on the platform of the N.B.C. concert hall, much to the consternation of the players of the brass and wood winds, all but lost in this forest of harps.

Richard Strauss mostly confines himself to the old-fashioned arpeggios, a surprising circumstance in view of his customary scoring ingenuity.

Mozart allows the harp wide range of expression in his Concerto for Flute and Harp:

Beethoven scored for it in his "Prometheus" music.

Several American composers have given the harp most generous treatment: Daniel Gregory Mason, in his Suite for Flute, Violin, Viola, Violoncello, and Harp; Timothy Mather Spelman in his Poem for Violin, Viola, Violoncello, Flute, and Harp; Nicolai Berezowsky in his Concerto for Harp; Paul Creston in his *Poeme;* Harl McDonald in his Suite from Childhood; Don Gillis in his Rhapsody; Paul White in his "Sea Chanty."

Expensive as the harp is (it retails at from $975 to $4,250), considerable as is its upkeep (strings cost from forty cents to $2.00 and periodic conditioning is desirable) and arduous as are its years of apprenticeship, it is not usually chosen by parents as an instrument to fill in Johnny's and Janie's idle hours. Harpists are serious individuals, with a determination to meet the requirements of a paid position, come fair, come stormy weather. You can be sure that the dulcet sounds you hear interweaving behind that radio program, giving the lift to that symphonic concert, holding the audience spellbound at a recital, are the result not of desultory flirting with the muse, but of a signed and sealed marriage contract with hard work, painstaking regular practice, with eyes held cool and unflinching on the goal.

## CHAPTER VI  -»» *The Guitar* «-

*Intimate and gentle are*
*The sounds made by the stringed guitar;*
*For serenades they'd surely please,*
*That is, if we had balconies.*

PEG BOX PEGS

FINGERBOARD

FRETS

SOUNDBOARD

SOUND HOLE

BRIDGE

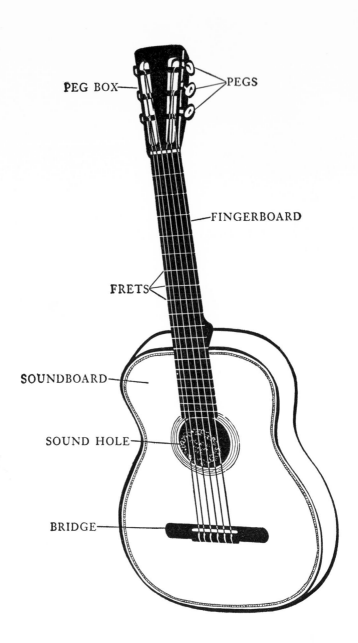

# THE GUITAR

THE guitar leads three separate existences whose borders scarcely overlap either in players, in literature, or in audiences. First, it flourishes in the great sunlit world of folk song and folk dancing. As an accompaniment to these, it is heard, especially in Spain, in Mexico, and in South America, in the streets, in the patios, at the races. The walls and ceilings of cafés are hung with patrons' guitars. Village dances go forward to the instrument's soft strumming. Peasants sing their songs to its harmonies. Serenades are embedded in its gentle chords. In the United States, it is played in many rural districts for square dances and for other get-togethers. Such guitars are often cheap affairs, the wood poor, the workmanship not too good, the accessories makeshift. Still, in the hands of their players, they become expressive instruments.

In its role in swing bands, the guitar is transformed into a percussive instrument. We shall speak of this aspect later.

Finally, there is the classic guitar of aristocratic lineage and impeccable workmanship. This is the instrument Paganini played expertly and seriously considered adopting for his career instead of the violin; the instrument Beethoven and Weber composed delightful works for; the instrument Berlioz mastered and taught for many years. Schubert played on it and sang his newly composed songs to its accompaniment. Domenico Scarlatti used it for its harmonic and rhythmic effects. Debussy studied it and utilized its resources. In the present day, Andrés Segovia has shown it to be on a par in tonal and technical resources with any musical instrument in the orchestra.

The music of the classic guitar is of an amazing expressiveness and variety. Vibrato, portamento, glissando, pizzicato, tremolo are interwoven in the execution of six-note chords, octaves, all intervals up to tenths, and on occasion much greater. Natural and artificial harmonics are produced in simple, double, and triple tones, with accompaniments simultaneously in the bass. Passages are possible in which the left hand both stops and sounds the string as well as "duet" passages between the two hands. Then there are "imitations"—harp tones, thin reedy metallic tones, snare-drum beats, bell tones, "tambour" effects. In short, infinite variations in polyphony, tone color, and dynamics are possible on this instrument. No wonder Hector Berlioz called it an orchestra in miniature!

It is not this virtuosity, however, that impresses the student when he first takes the guitar in his hands and holds it in playing position—that is, placed across his raised left knee (he is seated), his left foot supported by a low stool, his left hand over the fingerboard, his right hand over and at right angles to the strings. It is rather the instrument's extreme lightness, the comfort with which it is held, and the beauty of the single, simple tone.

The guitar has six strings sounded like this:

Note that the distance between neighboring strings is a fourth in every case except one, when it is a third. Note further that the highest and lowest strings are two octaves apart. The complete range for natural tones is a little over three octaves with an added octave obtained through artificial harmonics. Guitar music always is notated in the treble clef, and, for ease in reading, is written an octave higher than it actually sounds.

In the following example:

the upper row shows the notes the guitarist actually reads on the staff, while the lower rows show the notes actually heard.

Sometimes when the composition calls for a basic D, the guitarist temporarily tunes his lowest string, E, down one tone.

Fingering on the guitar is accomplished by four fingers of the left hand. The thumb should not be used to press down the strings (though under poor instruction it sometimes is) since it throws the hand out of gear. The right hand fingers—usually only four of them—pluck the strings. In melodic and contrapuntal playing (called *punteado*) the little finger is never used, though it does come into play in *rasgeado*, the rapid strumming of all strings by all fingers.

The classic guitar may be distinguished not only through its being completely hand-activated, but also through its construction. The fingerboard is broader than in the popular instrument, this so that the fingers may negotiate separate strings with ease. The rule is that the fingerboard be at least two inches wide at the point where it leaves the pegbox. Also, the twelfth fret on the classic guitar (the frets measure off semitones) comes exactly where the neck joins the body of the instrument. The fingerboard is absolutely flat (not curved as in the violin). The three upper strings are of nylon, the three lower of nylon wound with copper, or sometimes pure gold. The classic guitarist eschews steel strings, as he eschews the plectrum. Steel strings in any case would not do for an instrument so lightly constructed. The back of the guitar, unlike that of the violin, is absolutely flat.

The classic guitar differs also in internal construction. The stabilizing bars inside adopt a fan-shaped arrangement. Moreover the bridge, to which the strings are attached at the end away from the pegbox, is not embedded in the structure, but is glued to the outside, the strings just threaded through holes and looped under. In so delicately built an instrument this is found the best way to prevent the bridge from tearing away from the surface.

Since each specimen is handmade, the classic guitar offers unending opportunities for artwork. The wood, the
inlaying, the bridge, the neck, the fretwork, the ornamentation are all matters of deep study. Virtuosos such as
Emilio Pujoh, Ida Presti, Rey de la Torre, Vincente
Gomez, Vadah Olcott-Bickford, Olga Coelho, Terry
Usher, Richard S. Pick, not to mention Segovia, have instruments which in themselves are works of art.

No modern upstart, the classic guitar derives from a
multitude of medieval specimens which appeared under a
multitude of names. Standard instruments were then unknown. Each maker took pains to vary slightly each instrument he fashioned. Moreover, names were shifted
around, one instrument referred to under different names
in Spain and France, another pronounced the same but
spelled in any of several ways, according to who happened
to be writing about it—all resulting in a nomenclature that
is the despair of historians. A few facts, though, do come
out clearly. The lute:

shaped like a pear cut in half lengthwise, with a neck one-
fourth as long as the box and with fourteen or more
strings, contributed to the Spanish guitar its fretted fingerboard and the method of plucking the strings.

This instrument known in Europe since the seventh century when it was brought there from Arabia had, by the sixteenth century, developed into an orchestral instrument, with wide capabilities. Perhaps one reason for its disappearance was the care it required—it was estimated an eighty-year-old man had spent sixty of his years tuning the instrument—and the cost of its upkeep, on a par with the upkeep of a horse.

Another of the guitar's predecessors, the vihuela (known also as *chitarra latina*):

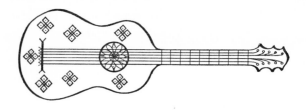

which held sway from the end of the fourteenth to the end of the sixteenth centuries, contributed to the guitar the curious pegbox construction (the pegs sticking out from behind the instrument), the system of tuning, and the general shape. Besides these instruments, there have been innumerable other variants—the cittern, the cister, the cither, the cithara, the gaifar, the tambur, the guiterna, the gittern, the gythorn, the guitra, the cistola, the citole and the cetera —to which we might add et cetera, et cetera, and let it go at that. The one stable quality of the early guitar, it seems, was its variability.

The tendency to vary still characterizes the instrument. Pass by any music store and you will see in the window,

beside rows of violins as neatly uniform as the quart bot-
tles placed along a milkman's route, guitars of fantastically
divergent types: with broad and narrow shoulders; with
steel strings and with nylon; with and without waistlines;
with narrow and wide necks; with flat and curved tops;
with strings extending the whole surface and with strings
stopping at the bridge; in sizes bass, tenor, and half; with
electric wires curling about them like snakes, and with
radiolike knobs embedded in their wood.

A few of the variants have taken on a certain stability.
The ukulele, for instance, which appeared in 1920 (imported from Hawaii which had in turn imported it from
Portugal) spread through the country like wildfire. In
shape of a miniature guitar, it had four strings, tuned so:

the first just one tone away from the last. This instrument,
fashioned to fill in the chinks and crannies between soprano, alto, tenor, and bass voices, has no solo aspirations.
Because of the ease with which it is learned, it makes an
excellent hobby instrument.

Much ukulele music is written in chord symbols. These
consist of diagrams of the frets with the "notes" indicated
where the fingers are to be placed on the fingerboard:

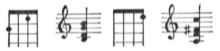

When open strings are sounded, no indication at all appears
on the diagram. This sort of notation really consists only

of finger directions with no designation as to harmonic or scale relationships. The reader is reading fingerings, not music. It does, however, have this to recommend it: even a player who does not read music, who has, in fact, no idea of key signatures, scales, accidentals, and such, can yet carry out the composers' intentions.

Unlike the modest ukulele, the steel guitar (also from Hawaii) is conspicuous wherever it is heard. It is played with a plectrum held in the right hand, and, held in the left, a little bar of steel that is oscillated on the desired fret, producing that wailing sound characteristic of Hawaiian music.

The mandolin:

a descendant of the lute and thus a cousin to the guitar, has four strings (or eight arranged in doubles) tuned exactly like a violin's. It is sounded by means of the rapid back-and-forth movement of a plectrum. It came to America from Spain around 1880, and by the turn of the century had become a fad, with 300,000 sold annually, and with mandolin clubs formed in most cities. It has received attention from great composers. Verdi employed it in his *Otello,* Mozart in his *Don Giovanni* and Mahler in his

Seventh Symphony. Beethoven wrote at least five pieces for mandolin and piano.

The banjo:

which was first heard on plantations in the South around 1825—it may have been copied after the *bania* of Senegambia, Africa—has from four to nine strings tuned in a variety of ways. This instrument, with a long neck and a body in the form of a parchment-covered drum open at the back, has such punctuating power that it held a prominent place in rhythm sections of jazz bands until the middle thirties, when the guitar crowded it out.

This brings us to the jazz guitar—heavier, larger, broader than the classic, electrically amplified, played with a plectrum, strung with steel strings. This is a true percussive instrument, its sound pulsing the swing band, giving it rhythmic stability. Since the six strings are sounded all at once by a plectrum and since the left hand often clamps around all strings at once, the narrow neck is an asset and is advertised as such. Advertisers also point with pride to such features as the "built-in tremolo," the "sharp treble," the "organ-stop control," and the "adjustable magnetic pickup." They list, moreover, "master-size guitars," "triangular guitars," and "triple-neck guitars"!

It is a far cry from these rhythm-rousers to the gentle tones of the classic guitar, and strange to realize that both categories are sold under the same general name. What with our age's blind thrust toward stridency, it is understandable that advocates of the classic guitar work with missionary zeal to further the cause of their instrument. Societies of the classic guitar have been formed in every country in the world, and a magazine, *The Guitar Review*, devoted to information on the subject, is published in New York.

None has been more zealous in championing its cause than Segovia. It is largely due to him that modern composers have written generously for the instrument. "I had to break the vicious circle in which it was closed," he told me recently. "There were no composers because there were no artists, and there were no artists because there were no composers. Now I have in my repertoire seven concertos written for guitar, two by Castelnuovo-Tedesco, one by Alexander Tansman, one by Joaquin Rodrigo, one by Villa-Lobos, one by Torroba, and one by Manuel Maria Ponce. Ponce has composed more than eighty works for guitar. These, along with those of Turina, Falla, and Manen, have given the guitar a status it has never before possessed."

But it is not only as stimulant to creative effort that Segovia has served the classic guitar. He has so fully demonstrated its possibilities that he has brought it back into the esteem it deserves. It is fortunate that he chose this instrument. He recently explained to me how this came about. "I was living in Granada," he told me, "a city in which the musical life was at a very low ebb. Yet my whole soul cried out for music. When I heard the guitar

—even as it was played on the street—the suavity of it, the nuances, the sonority, so captivated me, I gave myself up to that soft and nice-voiced instrument.

"I decided I would be an apostle of the guitar, or, to put it more exactly, her husband before God, swearing to provide her with the honor she deserved. I was my own teacher. I carefully studied piano exercises, noted how each made the fingers work and what degree of independence, strength, and agility it developed in them. Then I applied my observations to the technique of the guitar. I gave my first concert when I was fourteen. From that day to now I have never stopped."

*Part 2*

# »» WIND INSTRUMENTS ««

### FOREWORD

THE history of the modern wind instruments started, like
the story of the Garden of Eden, with a serpent:

This instrument was invented in the late sixteenth century
by a certain Guillaume, of Auxerre, France. Men had ex-
tracted music from pipes long before this, to be sure, but
this was the first successful attempt at so compressing the
pipe-length as to get the instrument within finger range.

Why get it within finger range?

To understand this, first think of a wind instrument as

exactly that—a *wind* instrument. Those coiled-pipe instruments in bands are only *coated* with brass. It is the column
of air inside that the player plays on. He plays on this air
by stirring it (with his breath) into ripples. The longer
the column of air, the wider the ripples, and the wider the
ripples, the lower the tone. So instruments with the greatest length of pipe (tubas, for instance) have the lowest
tones. The *quality* of the tone depends on the shape and
construction of the mouthpiece—cup-shaped, funnel-
shaped; on the type of reed—double (as in oboe, English
horn, bassoon, contra bassoon, bagpipe), single (as in
clarinet, saxophone); and on the shape of the air column,
that is, whether it widens out gradually or quickly and
whether it has a small bell or a large bell at the sound-
emitting end.

A column of wind, like a violin string, has harmonics.
By just changing the shape of the lips and breathing differently, one obtains, without fingering at all, the following harmonic progression:

One gets this progression, that is, if it's a C instrument—
if the instrument is built around that tone. The way you
would call a violin a G violin if it had only one string and
that string when twanged sounded the note G. An E-flat
instrument has the following progression:

and an F instrument the following:

Now notice those six holes in the sides of the serpent. Why should the player reach those six holes? Because otherwise the instrument would be capable of only *one* harmonic progression. Each hole adds to the number of harmonic progressions in the following fashion: when it is stopped it causes the air to shoot along instead of pouring out that vent, creating a longer column of air. The six finger holes thus make possible six more tones, each with its harmonic progressions, enough to fill out the whole chromatic scale along three octaves.

With this discovery of the function of holes in the wind instrument, the means of efficiently stopping them assumed paramount importance. Finger-stopping—just the bare fingers, that is—is haphazard at best, for any holes so small as to be stopped by the fingers are also too small to allow a full stream of air to escape.

This imperfection of the serpent worried one Halary of Paris, back at the beginning of the nineteenth century. After considerable cogitating he constructed a serpent with larger side holes and keys to cover them and called it the "keyed serpent," or ophicleide. Its principle of key-stopping has survived, in improved form, in, for instance, the clarinet which has padded metal tabs (keys) fitting over holes. Here is the ophicleide:

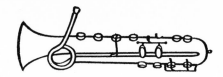

However, for brass wind instruments with their explosive air-projection, a more incisive way of hole-stopping was needed. Around the time of the battle of Waterloo (1815) the ophicleide, which had marched soldiers to the front in bands on both the English and French sides, gave way before the piston valve invented by Blümel—a valve that had every right to succeed. For it opened out new lengths in the instrument, made the air column longer. In an ordinary three-valve instrument, the player has at his disposal, in addition to the harmonic series natural to the instrument, six other series obtained by depressing the valves one at a time and in various combinations. A fourth valve makes available six additional harmonic series.

With this new incentive to accuracy and facility, whole families of instruments burgeoned out: cornets, saxhorns, trumpets, tubas. Those that have maintained their position in orchestras and bands of today are discussed in the following chapters.

Before reading these, though, we must understand transposition.

## CHAPTER VII

# TRANSPOSITION:
# MUSIC'S DOUBLE SOMERSAULT

THE symphony orchestra is about to begin its program. The conductor's baton is raised. It is Beethoven's *Egmont* Overture, and the opening phrase has all the instruments coming in on the same note, a mighty F. But wait a minute. Just take a look over the conductor's shoulder. The clarinet part is written like G; one trumpet (cornet) part has C printed there, and another trumpet has D. At least half of those instruments sounding F are reading other notes on the staff! Musical pandemonium? Not at all! They are all playing in perfect unison. And the conductor is nodding his approval.

At intermission time, ask the men if they were transposing for that first number. No, they will insist, they were reading the notes just as they stood on the staff. And they will be telling the truth. They were no more transposing than the clock on the mantelpiece pointing Daylight Saving Time is rushing the sun. It is the other way around. *The notation is transposing the instrument.*

"Imagine two pianos in one room," is the way *The Oxford Companion to Music** puts it, "and a composer who

* By Percy A. Scholes, published by Oxford University Press, quoted by permission.

· 73 ·

has to write music so that the two may be played together. He finds that one piano is at the normal pitch but that the other is (say) two semitones below that pitch. In copying out his music for the players, he therefore notates the part for the first piano normally and the part for the second, two semitones *higher*. The second piano has now become a 'transposing instrument', i.e., what the composer has transposed, on paper, from (say) key C to key D it transposes back, in sound, from key D to key C.

"Had the composer not transposed the second piano part up the player would have had to do so, and this, unless he were a very accomplished performer, might have hampered him every time he played the piece in giving due attention to the technical and expressional features of the music. It is better, then, that the composer should do the work for him once for all."

However, this is only part of the explanation.

"Why," one asks, "are those clarinets and those French horns and those trumpets, and the other 'transposing instruments' off pitch in the first place? What diabolical scheme makes half of the wind instruments give out sounds (with identical notation before them) from one to five tones apart from the other half?" Here is the story behind this situation:

Take the clarinets. A long time ago there was just one type of clarinet, not eight or so as there now are. The players on this instrument read music on the staff—music that looked just as it sounded, as music should—and got used to connecting their fingerwork with the notation. "All tone-holes covered," for instance, was synonymous with G. "One tone-hole open" was A. "Two tone-holes open" was B—and so on.

Then another clarinet was invented, longer and therefore deeper in tone, in fact, exactly one whole tone lower than the original clarinet. The inventor knew that, if he altered the tabs and holes that lined the instrument, clarinetists would never want to exchange their old familiar instrument for a new and strange one. So the inventor stuck to the same surface pattern and made his new clarinet look and finger like its higher-pitched predecessor. Sure enough, once the Bob Joneses and Pete Smiths of that day heard they could run up the scale without altering their fingering, they went off to buy themselves one of those new clarinets. But remember, this clarinet's compass was one tone lower. So when Jones and Smith played the old songs with friend Brown who had hung on to his old clarinet, the three sounded like cats caterwauling on the back fence. They decided these new instruments were a dead loss in ensemble playing.

But they reckoned without the composers.

For composers liked those deeper clarinets—liked the sound and range of them. They made up their minds if the players couldn't adjust their fingering, they, the composers, would adjust the notation. In other words, the scale, lowered a whole tone by the length of the instrument, would be jacked up again through notation. Thereafter a melody such as the following:

would appear in the clarinet part like this:

The clarinetist looked at that first note, D, and used the fingering he had always used for D on the old instrument. But, since his present clarinet was a tone lower in pitch than the one he had always played, the note *sounded* was C, just the note he was supposed to play. In short, like turning gloves inside-out to wash them and then turning them back to wear them, two changes got everything in order again. Transposing *via* notation an instrument already transposed *via* structure brought that instrument into harmony with the orchestral ensemble. As for the clarinet player, he was as tickled as the man who thought he wasn't gaining weight any more—"See, I can get two fingers inside my belt"—when all the time his wife was thoughtfully taking out the pleats to keep pace with his increasing poundage!

Inventors with an eye to sales and composers with an eye to performance were just as resourceful when it came to subsequent models. The inventors built them similar in fingering patterns to the initial ones (thus throwing the sound certain intervals off), while the composers regained the needed intervals *via* notation. If this was only a musical stop-gap, it did, like that arbitrary adjustment of the clock, Daylight Saving Time, conserve the midnight oil (those hours saved in practice!) and it did, also like Daylight Saving Time, keep all concerned working together in harmony.

There was still another reason for going along with this improvisational trick. It aided when the players had to switch instruments frequently. Take the saxophone family for illustration. There are five members of this group in frequent use, with the following ranges:

Each player switches around from one to another, sometimes once or twice in the course of a single composition. Consider what confusion there would be if he had to switch music, too—or think in other finger patterns. As it is, the notation for each of these instruments, from the high-voiced B-flat soprano to the low-voiced B-flat bass, is written so:

A player on any one of the instruments, looking at, say

presses down the left index finger, and looking at:

presses down all eight fingers. No variation. No shifting of gears. No "transposing." The transposing is done through the notation itself.

This situation holds true of the trumpet, or the horn—

of all "transposing instruments," in fact. In a sort of benign pact, inventor and composer have done all the transposing for the instrumentalist.

Thus the composer takes the following shifts into account:

This note (C) written on the staff:

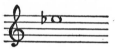

sounds, for the piccolo in D♭:

for the E♭ clarinet:

for the B♭ clarinet,
B♭ soprano saxophone,
B♭ trumpet (cornet):

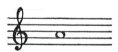

for the A clarinet,
A trumpet (cornet):

for the Alto flute in G:

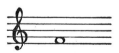

for the English horn,
French horn (in F):

for the E♭ alto clarinet,
E♭ alto saxophone,
E♭ alto horn or melophone:

for the baritone,
B♭ tenor saxophone,
B♭ bass clarinet:

for the E♭ baritone saxophone:

for the B♭ bass saxophone:

There is one slight flaw in this let-the-composer-do-it attitude. Music for clarinet or saxophone or trumpet or some other transposing instrument is not always available. A saxophonist may be called on to read from viola music; or a trumpet may be asked to read music from a piano part. Or a horn may get tangled up in untransposed editions of one kind or another. Then saxophonist or trumpet player or horn player must transpose *on the spot* all that notation —transpose often not just up the comfortable whole tone but up and down fourths and fifths.

The trumpet and horn seem to be the hardest hit in this regard. The trumpet, for instance, because it was a long time growing up, has a great deal of music with which it has to contend, written for the simple one-scale bugle. Bach's and Handel's and Mozart's music is so scored. Even composers of recent times have written for trumpet as though it could play only one scale. Some modernists have made near chaos of this confusion by writing in several different ways for trumpet *in a single composition.* In such cases instrumentalists themselves have to take up the slack.

Of course in dance bands there are the arrangers whose job it is to smooth the instrumentalist's path. In the larger concert bands, too, arrangers step into the breach, save the instrumentalists from the hazards of transposing. It is the smaller ensembles with limited budgets who suffer most. Or that lone accompanist who is asked by the nervous soprano to "Please play 'Kiss Me Again' down one semi-tone—I'm out of voice tonight!"

All instrumentalists, in short, whether accompanists, or members of small town or top-flight orchestras, have learned never to grow placid in the belief they need play only what is set before them. For sure as sure will come the day when a fevered conductor will lean over his stand and whisper hoarsely, "The Mayor of Oshkosh likes 'The Star-Spangled Banner' played in G. Just transpose it down a tone and a half, men!"

## CHAPTER VIII

⟫ *The Tuba* ⟪

*Tubas are quite short on buyers,*
*Make a fourth in most trombonist choirs,*
*For solos they're rare,*
*But at times have a flair*
*For revealing their innermost fires.*

*In bands to avoid a neurosis*
*They take on a metamorphosis,*
*As euphoniums, sousaphones,*
*Tenors and baritones*
*Sound forth in generous doses.*

THE DOUBLE-BELLED EUPHONIUM

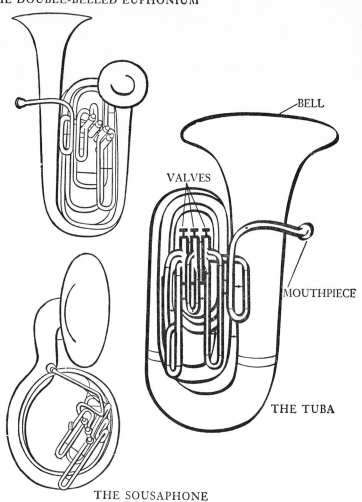

BELL

VALVES

MOUTHPIECE

THE TUBA

THE SOUSAPHONE

# THE TUBA

IF YOU could stretch out the tuba's shiny brass coiling, it would measure about thirty-five feet. The tuba provides the deepest brass tones in the orchestra and is to it what the pedal pipes are to the organ. Wagner, Richard Strauss, and Stravinsky have taken to it. They use it as the bass of the brass quartet (the other three members are trombones), as a fifth horn, and as a reinforcement for the bass viol section. It also has heavy responsibilities in bands, taking the place of bass viols there. Besides, little boys love it, it's so big and shiny and its bell is so good for chucking paper wads into as it goes gaily by in parades.

Essential both to orchestras and bands, tubas, at least in appearance, are quite different species in these two organizations. Since Sousa's time, the instrument he invented, the sousaphone, is the type of tuba predominantly used in bands. The orchestral tuba is more compact and may have an upturned bell, as in the illustration opposite, or a bell turned out. The latter is often called a recording tuba since it has a more directive sound.

A tuba player in an orchestra owns sometimes as many as five of these instruments in various sizes: the C tuba, the B-flat tuba, the E-flat tuba, the F tuba, the tenor tuba. (Such designations as C, B-flat, and E-flat indicate the instrument's "open" tone—the one that sounds when a player blows into it without keying or lipping.) The smaller the instrument, the higher the range. Here are the ranges of those named:

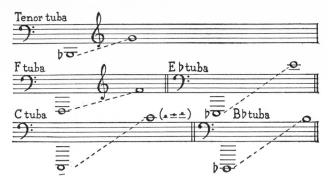

Symphony orchestra players, most of them, play regularly on the C tuba. It covers the range ordinarily required and, all things considered, is easiest to play.

Orchestral tubas may be further classified according to whether they have buttons, which control piston valves, or levers, which control rotary valves. Both devices are the means of opening extra lengths of tubing. The piston type of mechanism is, as a rule, quieter and easier to control. With it, the glissando is easier to produce effectively. A tuba player who uses the rotary valve type usually shifts to the piston type for the famous glissando in Strauss's *Don Quixote*.

This is what the buttons or levers actually do: Say you are sounding the "open" tone. Now press the second valve and the open tone becomes a half-tone lower. Release this second valve and press the first valve and the sound lowers another half-tone. (Now you're a tone lower than the open tone.) Next, press the first and second valves to-

gether *or* press the third valve alone, and you get three
half-tones down from the open tone. Now press the third
valve plus the second and you have four half-tones down
from the open tone. *Five* half-tones down is obtained by
your pressing simultaneously the first valve and the third;
six half-tones by pressing down the first three valves together. This, incidentally, is the limit of the three-valve
instrument. Symphony tubas invariably have *four* keys
or levers. The fourth pressed down in various combinations with the other three makes it possible to sound four
more half-tones. These half-tones and the tones obtained
by lipping (embouchure) and by altering the flow of
breath, form the whole range of the instrument.

During an orchestral concert, the tuba player blows into
his instrument a good part of the time. Since there is
usually only one tuba in an orchestra, he mustn't break
down. In a few compositions in which two tubas are
needed, a second is employed temporarily. The orchestral
player may be called on to use four tubas at a single concert. He sometimes changes instruments in the course of
a composition, in Berlioz' *Romeo and Juliet*, for instance,
and in Stravinsky's *Pétrouchka* for the famous "bear" solo:

Incidentally this passage, often used for audition purposes,
has probably won and lost more jobs for tuba players than
any other passage in their repertoire.

Kleinsinger's *Tubby the Tuba*, that drama of the under-dog who finally comes into his own, gives the tuba solo status throughout. When Joseph Novotny played it with the Houston Symphony Orchestra several seasons ago (he was a member of that orchestra then) he forthwith became a celebrity, at least within all public school precincts of the city. Shrill voices pursued him everywhere. "There goes Tubby! Good old Tubby!" Teachers remarked that in the free drawing period, tubas took precedence over bunnies, witches, and supermen. The year-end compositions that the boys and girls wrote on "Why I Like My Orchestra" gave one the impression that the glowing tuba *was* the orchestra.

In symphony orchestras, besides sounding with three trombones as a "choir," in such a passage as:

RIDE OF THE VALKYRIES

when a majestic choral effect is required, and doubling with second tuba or trombone in such a passage as Strauss's *Also sprach Zarathustra:*

it comes out with solo force in such a passage as the following from Wagner's *Faust* Overture:

Once in one of Toscanini's turbulent rehearsals, when the tuba was playing this passage, the Maestro paused in his vehement onrush, laid down his baton and quietly asked his tuba player to "Please play that passage again." When he had finished it, Toscanini said, "Now please play it once again!" and then, at the end, "Still another time, please." Finally the tuba player (it was William Bell of the New York Philharmonic Symphony) asked him what there was to correct.

"Nothing," said Mr. Toscanini. "Only I never heard anything so beautiful."

In concert bands, tubas have special responsibilities, for here they uphold what in the symphony orchestra would constitute the bass viol section. Sousa's band had five and, on occasion, six tubas. Concert bands today use one tuba ordinarily for every twelve players. A forty-eight-piece band thus has four tubas, and they usually play in unison.

However, tubas, as symphony patrons know them, scarcely ever appear in professional bands. If Paul Lavalle, conductor of the Band of America, would ask his tuba section to stand up during, say, their rendition of that famous passage in the band arrangement of César Franck's Symphony in D minor:

sousaphone players Tarto, Butterfield, Corrado, and Jen-kel would spring to their feet. Sousaphones—these are simply tubas with the tubes twisted differently—are so recent an acquisition to the world of instruments that they just barely got a look-in on the nineteenth century. It was in 1898 that they first appeared, and it was Sousa who first used them. Let that great bandmaster himself tell it through the pages of his autobiography, *Marching Along:* "I strove in every way to improve the quality and variety of the instrument [tuba]. Way back when I was with the Marines they used a helicon tuba wound around the body. I disliked it for concert work, because the tone would shoot ahead and be too violent. I suggested to a manufacturer that we have an upright bell of large size so that the sound would diffuse over the entire band like the frostiness on a cake! He designed a horn after that description, and it has been in use ever since by many bands, under the name of the sousaphone."

The sousaphone underwent a slight modification in 1908 when the bell was turned front. Sousa, however, con-tinued with the old type throughout his life. For one further proof that the manner of coiling has nothing to do with the sound of the instrument—there's another bass tuba, an elongated one, standing higher than a man, created for the Band of America. In tone, in range, in fingering, it is exactly like the other tubas.

Suggestive of the tubas in their manner of tapering are the euphonium and the baritone, cellos in the band just as the tubas are the bass viols. Unlike the tubas baritones and euphoniums are practically never used in orchestras.

The baritone has a compass of two and one-half octaves, though if players have a strong embouchure higher and lower notes can be played:

The euphonium, almost a twin to the baritone, has as distinguishing qualities a wider bore that gives it greater volume and mellowness in the lower notes. Its extra valve (it has four) lowers its compass by an augmented fourth. Its range is:

The euphonium has sired a particularly interesting offspring, the double-belled euphonium. Notice its Siamese-twin-like proportions in the illustration on page 82.

Notice, too, that it is, in fact, two separate and distinct instruments with two separate coilings; two separate bells (the small bell imitating the tenor voice, the large one the baritone voice); two apportionments of valves (the fifth valve opens the smaller bell); and, as one uniting feature, a single mouthpiece. No, it cannot play duets with itself!

One would like to speculate on what new instruments may spring forth from this most prolific group. We already hear of a tuba that can be played by two instrumentalists at once, and one that coils rather terrifyingly around the neck. One thing is certain. Instruments as necessary to the welfare of our large ensembles as tubas, sousaphones, baritones, and euphoniums will never be let alone by inventive musicians until they are perfection itself.

## CHAPTER IX

»» *The French Horn* ««

*The French horn's sensitive; it's rumored*
*Its scale has notes which must be humored.*
*The players are a helpful team,*
*So all comes out as smooth as cream.*

# THE FRENCH HORN

WHEN Siegfried's horn call sounds out clear and strong over an orchestra a-murmur with forest sounds; when the great aria of Leonora in *Fidelio* comes wreathed in rich horn tones; when Mendelssohn's *Midsummer Night's Dream* Nocturne emerges serene through orchestral ripplings—do not for a moment think those four (or more) players sitting up there behind their circular shiny instruments—the French horn is sometimes aligned with the brass, sometimes with the wood winds—are basking in the beauty of their tones. They are not basking. They are sweating. They are wondering if that ice water they drank ten minutes before is going to queer that opening note in *Oberon*. If they shouldn't have eaten that steak after rather than before the concert. If they hadn't practiced too much that day and tired their lips. If they hadn't practiced too little and lost their embouchure. If that fortissimo attack isn't going to spoil their playing in the piano passage. If they are going to overblow the *Eulenspiegel* motif as a reaction from the pianissimo. If their buddies in the horn section can be depended on or if *they* have eaten steaks or drunk ice water or practiced too much or too little.

Improvements in the French horn have by no means improved the lot of the player. Of course now he does not have to carry around that bagful of shiny crooks, such as used to clank against French horn players' shins in the old days, doesn't have to slip them onto his arm at concert and slide them off one by one as the program progresses. All he trundles about now is an extra mouthpiece, funnel-shaped, very small, the smallest of any, in fact, in the orchestra. And of course that problem child of his, the sixteen-foot-, or so, long tube of brass twisted into a confusion of coils and flaring out in a wide bell at the end—his horn.

Don't think the problem consists, either, in just keeping that horn polished and cleaned, in not dropping or denting it, or in seeing it isn't freezing cold or sun-baked at concert-time (either would put the tone off). The real problem has to do with the horn's inner self—its soul, so to speak. For the French horn doesn't, for all its improvements, play an even scale. The player has to humor it in its weak spots, has to avoid breaks. And it can make a mighty nasty sound if it is improperly muted.

About that muting . . .

Mutes can be bought at the store in great variety, made of wood, cardboard, metal, papier-mâché, and so on. Each has its special tonal characteristic. Each has special passages to interpret. But just because mutes *are* so specialized, they don't quite fill the bill. Most players prefer the more adjustable and versatile way of muting their horns, that is, by inserting their right hand in the bell (their left is occupied with fingering). This, according to the way they hold the hand (1) softens or makes louder the tones; (2) raises or lowers, by at least a semitone, the pitch; (3) gets those recalcitrant notes into scale-line; (4) gives, when the bell is almost completely sealed and the player blowing softly, the quality of remoteness; and (5) obtains, when the bell is altogether sealed—well, almost altogether —and the player still blowing hard, a nasal quality not exactly delightful but often useful (for instance, in *Till Eulenspiegel's Merry Pranks*). Besides all this, the hand steadies the instrument.

If it is a problem child in the practice room, the French horn develops a real neurosis when lined up with its fellows on the concert platform. French horns have a tendency to stand out even when they should blend in. Horn players—four are required in every symphony orchestra— have to learn to work together with the persistency and selflessness of ants. They must imagine they are a football team and interweave harmonies the way backfield men pass the ball. They must imagine they are a squad of firemen and make the hose—or rather, the melody—draw out a smooth length. They must imagine they are pats of glowing paint on an easel and not spread themselves on too thick.

Probably because of this necessity for cooperative effort, French horn players display a fraternal feeling rare even among instrumentalists. Of the five interviewed for this book—James Stagliano, Frank Brouk, Arthur Berv, James Chambers, and Mason Jones, respectively of the Boston, Cleveland, N.B.C., New York, and Philadelphia orchestras —each showed a high regard for his fellow horn players, as experts on this, one of the most difficult instruments in the orchestra.

Of the cooperative foursome appearing in most symphony orchestras, the first and third horns take the high passages, and the second and fourth horns the low. Just like belonging to the Episcopal clergy—you're either "high" or "low" and, once so, you usually stay that way for life.

Even "double-horn" players stick to the high and low categories. Double horns are horns that are so constructed with two sections of pipes that they can shift gears, so to speak, pass, like the man of flying trapeze fame, with the greatest of ease back and forth between high and low ranges. The shift is made by the left thumb pressing down a lever or key (this behind the outside row of three finger keys) thus diverting the horn from the F channel (warm, velvety, and therefore better in low registers) to the B-flat channel (brilliant and therefore better in high registers). Such a double horn goes:

Solo horn players, by which we mean those who in orchestras are assigned the outstanding passages, use the double horn (rather than the ordinary single-valve horn) since it is more versatile.

Sometimes it is just too versatile for the player's stamina and he wishes the horn were back in the days when it was simply that—a ram's horn with a hole in the pointed end, capable of sounding one nice, clear tone with no fingering, no tonguing, and no breaks. He wishes this when he has to play the Mendelssohn Nocturne right after a Strauss *Eulenspiegel* theme, and then top that off with a Stravinsky

*Firebird* arpeggio. To make his lot at least endurable the custom has arisen for symphony orchestras to employ alternates or assistants, especially at the first or solo horn desks. Some orchestras—Boston's and Dallas', for instance —have alternates for each of the four horn-player desks— eight horn players in all.

So now we have our French horn section exuding serenity in Weber's *Der Freischütz* Overture, registering exuberance in Strauss's *Don Juan*, snarling defiance in Tchaikovsky's Sixth Symphony, mirroring daybreak in the second act of *Götterdämmerung*, and crying alarm in Dukas' *Sorcerer's Apprentice*. We say we have them. That is more than the conductor can say. Hard to get and hard to keep, horn players are the cherished darlings of their conductors. And, once a conductor has four good horn players, he adopts every wile to keep them, even to making them the highest paid members of his orchestra.

But, since men who have had the tenacity to perfect themselves on this more-than-ordinarily difficult instrument are by no means fly-by-nighters, we have the situation of horn players, once they are established in their symphony orchestras, continuing for over a quarter of a century in one orchestra, as did that solo horn player of the Philadelphia Orchestra, the venerable Anton Horner, who, incidentally, is said to have been also the teacher of more than half of the French horn players in our country's greatest orchestras. In this age of quick turnover and instability of purpose, it is a record worthy of citation both for him and for his many pupils.

CHAPTER X  →» *The Trombone* «←

*The slide, for trombones, is the means*
*For playing highs, lows, in betweens;*
*Their dignity will not permit*
*Glissandos save in jazz a bit.*

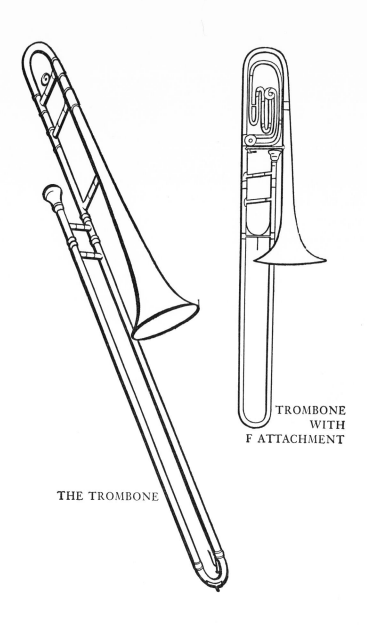

TROMBONE
WITH
F ATTACHMENT

THE TROMBONE

# THE TROMBONE

I ONCE spent half an hour passing along the corridors of the six floors of the Juilliard School of Music in New York, ear cocked toward one door after another, listening for trombone sounds—this when I had gone there to interview Roger Smith, teacher of the instrument. Piano, strings, and percussion were passed up after a single chord or clash. But that sound, veiled and soothing? An oboe, probably. And that, nasal and sinuous? A saxophone, maybe. And that, brilliant and metallic? A trumpet, no doubt. Door after door, past muffled staccatos, shivering arpeggios, incisive triads, tenuous legatos. And then suddenly something like a voice, but fuller. Tone noble and sonorous. Dignified. I thought of those balconies of the Middle Ages, where the evening hour was ushered in by a choir of instruments. I thought of dim-aisled cathedrals, of pilgrims marching, of angels chanting. I thought of trombones. I walked in.

The trombone's history goes way, way back. In fact, it is the only instrument that has from the beginning of the modern era (circa 1500) to the present time retained its essential characteristics. The Italian painter, Matteo di Giovanni, whose death occurred in 1495, depicted the first trombone in modern form. (Since the bell did not expand so widely, it probably had a "chamber-music" tone.) By the middle of the sixteenth century these instruments were playing chorales from the towers, and, at street level, were enlivening wedding receptions, festivals, state occasions. They accompanied at church services, too.

This instrument which has played so dramatic a role throughout the years is simple enough in structure. Two-thirds of its length is made up of cylindrical tubing, the remaining third of gradual expansion of the bell. It operates, like all other wind instruments, on the longer-the-pipe-the-deeper-the-tone principle. Some clever Italian, working with the tuning slide of his trumpet back in the fourteenth century, discovered that shoving in the slide raised the sound a whole tone, and thereby hit upon a way of forming a scale accurate in pitch and comparatively easy to negotiate. So the trombone, conditioned in its intonation entirely by the player's sense of pitch—with no valves and no keys—was evolved.

Don't get the idea, though, that the more than three octaves the trombone encompasses mean thirty-odd stops for semitones up the length of the slide. It's not so simple as that. Only *seven* semitones are arrived at by the process of sliding out the trombone (in the early trombone there were but four semitones). These seven haiting places are called positions. (The first position is with the slide closed. Each nudge outward of the U-pipe lowers the tone by a semitone.)

Other notes than these seven semitones are produced by various manipulations of the breath supply and lips. The positions produce, directly and *via* harmonics, the following notes:

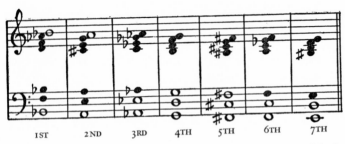

| 1ST | 2ND | 3RD | 4TH | 5TH | 6TH | 7TH |

The practical compass of the instrument is as in *A* below. The "pedal" tones (see *B* below) are hard to produce and rarely used:

Because it has its basis in harmonic rather than in scale sequence, the trombone doesn't thrive on fast-moving parts or on passages that require quick changes in direction. Composers who do call for this "bicycle pump" technique just aren't scoring properly for the instrument. Since the player's tonal judgment is the sole guide to correct playing, a trombonist without a good ear is a contradiction in terms. A pianist or a guitarist (the former has keys to demarcate the tone, the latter has frets) might get by for a time at least with but a hazy sense of pitch. Not so a trombonist. He has to know his semitones as a mother knows her children. Legato offers the trombonist some difficulty, too. He masters it through careful control of his breath, thus covering the halt required between notes to allow for shifting of the slide. This "invisible" method of bridging the gap between two notes is often called portamento. Glissando is another story. The trombone can do glissando fine!

The special tone color of the trombone—dignified, solemn, rich, and smooth—is attributable in part at least to the mouthpiece, which is larger than that of the trumpet. (The trombone is considered the bass of the trumpet.) The trombone is capable of a tremendous tone, when the player gives it full wind. It can also produce a barely audible pianissimo.

The trombone hasn't any flaws in its structure. Well, *hardly* any. There's that little matter of the outer moving slide being just a bit larger than the inner one over which it works. Because of this, some notes have a tendency to "break" and have to be essayed rather carefully.

About holding the instrument: The left hand, held at the juncture of the bell and slide, near the mouthpiece, bears the weight and steadies the instrument, while the right hand manipulates the slide. The trombone requires much less care than, say, the reed instruments. Some players lubricate the slide with facial cream. They maintain that it stays on longer than oil. Some use a special spray. In any case, they have to clean it all off every week and put on a new application.

Trombones come in various sizes. Those principally in use in our symphony orchestras are the tenor trombone (see range in foregoing example) and the bass trombone. The bass instrument has a larger bore (diameter of tubing), a larger bell, and a larger mouthpiece. Also it almost invariably has an F attachment. What actually happens in such an instrument is this: you push your left thumb on what is called the thumb key, and it turns a little rotary valve that gives access to about four feet (bent around) of extra tubing, the F valve. Among other advantages this extra tubing releases the four notes between the lower E and the pedal notes:

The ranges of the bass and the tenor trombones are otherwise the same. The F attachment appears often in tenor trombones, too. In fact, any trombone can be fitted with one. Trombones that play for opera, with their added responsibilities, have it almost of necessity. About one-third of symphony trombones have it.

Gluck, by writing for trombones (in his "Divinités du Styx") in three parts, established a custom adhered to down to the present day. Bach never allowed it a solo part as he did practically every other instrument. The statue music in Mozart's opera, *Don Giovanni*, scores for a choir of three trombones, one of them supplying the melody, the others the background. Beethoven, when he wanted to give a sense of vast jubilant strength in the last movement of his Fifth Symphony, brought in the trombones, adding them to the sum total of all the other instruments. He used them also to marvelous effect in his Sixth and Ninth.

Schubert used the trombone in his later symphonies. A fine example of its possibilities as a solo instrument appears in the last movement of his C-major Symphony. Weber showed (in his operas) what wonders it could perform in soft harmony.

Hector Berlioz, more than any other, was responsible

for the trombone's full use. He continually shouted its praises. "It can chant like a choir of priests," he wrote. "It can threaten, lament, ring a funeral knell, raise a hymn of glory, break forth into frantic cries or sound its dread flourish to awaken the dead or to rouse the living." In his *Symphonie funèbre et triomphale* the "Funeral Oration" is entrusted largely to the solo trombone. He employed the difficult pedal notes for special effects in his *Requiem.*

Wagner was another intelligent champion of the trombone. He brought out its dignified parade tone in the "Chorus of the Pilgrims" in his *Tannhäuser* Overture and underlined its intensely dramatic qualities in the Prelude to Act III of *Lohengrin:*

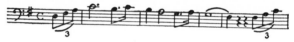

The solemn compact between Wotan and the Giants in the second scene of *Das Rheingold* is carried through to the tones of trombones playing in stirring unison.

Brahms used trombones in his choral works and symphonies. The theme:

from the Finale of his First Symphony in C minor shows how trombones may be made to sound out like magnificent, sonorous voices.

Symphony orchestras today usually employ at least three trombones: two tenors and a bass. Modern composers use them more for special effects, less for bolstering up other instruments. Prokofiev uses glissando in his "Cinderella" ballet. Stravinsky in his Violin Concerto and *Symphony of Psalms* scored for a single trombone to relieve the monotony of double basses and cellos played in octaves.

Trombones are all but indispensable in swing orchestras, but you'd hardly know them for the same instrument there. Perhaps on the same principle as a Puritan making a right about face to Bohemianism, the trombone in its jazz phase goes in for the very things it is not supposed to do in symphony orchestras. Listen to its sardonic scooping. Listen to its blaring, its raucous comments. Listen to it upsetting every convention, snorting down every credo. It thrusts in a mute and projects an entirely new tone. It gives a vibrato. It *slides* a vibrato. It travels in the high regions incognito as a trumpet. It punctuates melody with hilarious gulps. It oozes the bluest of blues. In short, the "push pipe" is to modern jazz what the Pan's pipes are to the primitive pastorale. It sets the tone. It *is* the thing.

A certain amount of bemoaning is heard in symphonic camps regarding the "cheapening" effects of the jazz trombonist, but the more thoughtful members of the classical contingency admit that the technical advances of the jazz player have brought symphonic players to their toes, have made modern composers score more rigorously with greater reliance on the trombonist's technical facilities.

## CHAPTER XI  »» *The Trumpet* ««

*It tingles spines, it shivers walls;*
*It's used for sports and battle calls;*
*As children's toy it's painted red;*
*In Gabriel's hands it wakes the dead.*

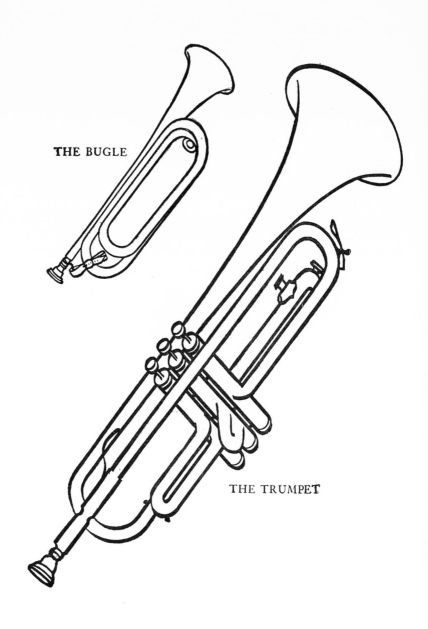

THE BUGLE

THE TRUMPET

# THE TRUMPET

THROUGH the ages the trumpet has changed in shape dozens of times—long, curved, doubled on itself, crooks added, valves added. Its uses, moreover, have been legion. Through it all, though, it is able, and has always been able, to play *loud*. It can be heard all over the place. In Old Testament days—it was a long straight tube then with a conical bell—it called warriors to battle, and today, as a bugle, it still shows its power by getting soldiers out of bed on freezing mornings. Four centuries before the Christian era athletes at the Olympic games entered trumpet contests to test their lung power. Queen Elizabeth I had twelve trumpets play a half hour before dinner to summon courtiers from her vast palace grounds. When stagecoaches brought the mail to outlying regions, post horns sounded out notice of their approach so that the villagers could foregather.

The trumpet has not only loudness. It has *directed* loudness. In the old days when it was still that long tube, the player turned the bell toward the point of desired contact and, whether that point was inches or miles away, the sound reached. Old prints show heralds, with banners suspended from their extended trumpets, announcing to assembled multitudes the approach of royalty. Bas-reliefs and tapestries present angels, their cheeks distended like apples, pointing their trumpets down toward the unregenerate earth in a fervor of proselytizing. And, to come down to the present, notice the race-track trumpeters sounding their "Boots and Saddles" for a whole stadium of listeners.

The long, unwound trumpet was for centuries the only type known. Then some thoughtful soul, probably noticing what a wind-lashing the instrument was taking and how the earth's gravitation was pulling it down, conceived the idea of winding it round and round on itself. The instrument so evolved we know today as the bugle. Playing this was just as simple as playing the long trumpet. You just blew the "natural" tone into it and then changed the tension of the lips to get that tone's overtones.

But this lack of a straight scale set inventive minds to working again. Such a fine-sounding instrument ought to be able to play anything. So in the seventeenth and eighteenth centuries, we find a *tromba da tirarsi*, a trumpet with a slide like a trombone, able to negotiate even chromatic notes. Also, someone around the seventeenth century added crooks, *U*-shaped contrivances fitted into the pipe of the trumpet which pulled out long or pushed in short, thus lowering or raising the tone. But the player had to stop playing to change them; and, also, they simply shifted the "natural" tone and its series of overtones. He still couldn't play a straight scale from bottom to top.

Around the turn of the nineteenth century came the valve trumpet, in which lengths of pipe could be opened by pressing buttons. By this procedure enough semitones were provided to produce a full scale.

The routine is as follows: press the first button (counting from the player) and you lower the pitch by two semitones; press the second button and it goes down one
semitone; the third, three semitones. By pressing two buttons in various combinations as well as the three together,
the initial tone is lowered by four, five, or six semitones.
Thus are achieved all the notes in the scale. Change in
breath pressure and lipping produces the higher octaves.

It becomes clear that most of the wind instruments are
so constructed that all notes do not sound with equal ease,
as they do on the piano, but rather that a certain harmonic
series is favored. Moreover, the instrument is named after
the fundamental of the series it thus favors, just as one
might call the toy horn of a child after the tone it produces
when it is simply blown into. Samuel G. Krauss, first
trumpet player of the Philadelphia Orchestra, uses, as occasion requires, five trumpets: a B-flat, a C, a D, an E-flat,
and an F. The B-flat instrument—the standard one in most
orchestras—can be altered to play like an A instrument by
extending the tuning slide, a little crook at one of the
U-turns of the instrument. Professionals, however, do not
use this in ordinary playing, since it tends to throw the
instrument slightly out of intonational balance. Instead, in
short passages when the key changes but when changing
instruments would be embarrassing, they continue to play
in the key which is natural to their instrument but transpose (see chapter on transposition) the notes—they sound
an A when they read a B-flat, and so on.

Trumpet players normally switch around from one to
another instrument as need requires, depending on which

fits the compositions played. The C, for instance, has an especially brilliant sound and can get around in the higher ranges easily. Each has its own peculiar assets, yet each is a complete and competent instrument, with a dependable range and a quick, smooth way of responding to the *taka taka ta* and the *ta ta ka ta* of the expert player.

Symphony and opera composers call for the trumpet when they want the audience to feel the prickle up the spine, to hear the crack of doom, to sense onrushing armies. They use trumpets for a curtain raiser, a fanfare, a prelude to a proclamation. They employ them to provide a sense of pageantry. Beethoven scored for them tellingly in the dungeon scene of Act II of his opera *Fidelio* when they signal to Pizarro that the Minister is coming. It is the climax of the scene, and the trumpet call is intensely dramatic:

Verdi employed trumpets with brilliant effect in the triumphal march of the troops in *Aïda*, Act II, Scene 2:

Composers, such as Haydn, Mozart, Mendelssohn, Wagner, use the trumpet for stirring sonority, a firm background harmony, mellow yet strong. Thus we find it in Wagner's *Lohengrin* Prelude:

Its brightness is heard in Mendelssohn's "Wedding March":

Its pianissimo, quite as beautiful as that produced by any other instrument in the orchestra, is heard in the D trumpet part of Stravinsky's *Symphony of Psalms,* in which the trumpet plays up to a high D in a whisper.

If a composer wants to express majesty in miniature, grandiosity gone haywire, he calls for the trumpet mute, a pear-shaped device inserted in the bell. Wagner did this in the last act of *Die Meistersinger* to imitate the tiny trumpets of the Guild of Tailors:

It is similarly used in the *Samuel Goldenberg and Schmuyle* section of the Moussorgsky-Ravel *Pictures at an Exposition:*

Richard Strauss was one of the first to write chromatically for the instrument. His gift for utilizing its full tonal palette is demonstrated particularly in his operas *Salome* and *Elektra*.

The opera orchestra trumpeter has special problems, as Isidor Blank of the Metropolitan Opera Orchestra pointed out to me. "We have to adjust our playing to the individual singers so that proper balance is maintained. Besides the trumpets are on stage as well as off, and the trumpeters have to see that there is a perfect merging between them. *Aïda*, for instance, has eleven trumpets on stage and two trumpets in the orchestra proper. *Die Meistersinger* has ten trumpets on stage. *Lohengrin* has eight trumpets on one side of the house and four on the other, with three in the orchestra—fifteen in all! It's some job to get all *those* synchronized!"

The trumpet and jazz may not have been made for each other, but they certainly hit it off from first acquaintanceship. Jazz's blatancy, its piercing urgency, its versatility, and its dramatic flair are the trumpet's own. Jazzists sensed this. Louis Armstrong, counted by many the greatest of all jazz players, is a trumpeter as are scores of others who have reached the top rung. Since good jazz players are all improvisers, they find the trumpet—with its overtones stretching out in tantalizing vistas and its scales going modern on the slightest provocation—the perfect setup for personal adventuring. Besides, there are the alterations in tone made possible by means of the mutes—the "wa-wa," the "growl," the "plunger," and whatever else ingenuity thinks up—not to mention the half-lowered piston which produces muffled sounds. Then there are the cleaving of sound waves and the splitting of eardrums in the above-the-staff notes, stuff for strong lungs and iron lips.

A word of caution here. Young players, trying to emulate their jazz idols' technical feats in the high registers, may force their lips prematurely and thus ruin their embouchures. Stentorian playing should be reserved for full maturity.

Sometimes it is not so much the lip that gets spoiled. It is the point of view. Young people who become too eager for display are no longer willing to take the hard, slow way to technical mastery.

Perhaps the true secret of the trumpet's success in the jazz field, though, is its ability to sound like the human voice—hysterical, ecstatic, or just plain blue. A "hot" player can imitate these human tones with an amazing variety of timbre. And since he produces vibrations in trumpet tone through an extension of vibrations in his own body, he finds his medium both flexible and responsive. As Armstrong once said to me: "Me and my horn, we know each other. We know what we can do. When I'm blowing, it's like me and my horn are the same thing."

## CHAPTER XII　⋙ *The Bassoon* ⋘

*Most useful is the deep bassoon*
*Although it seldom carries a tune.*

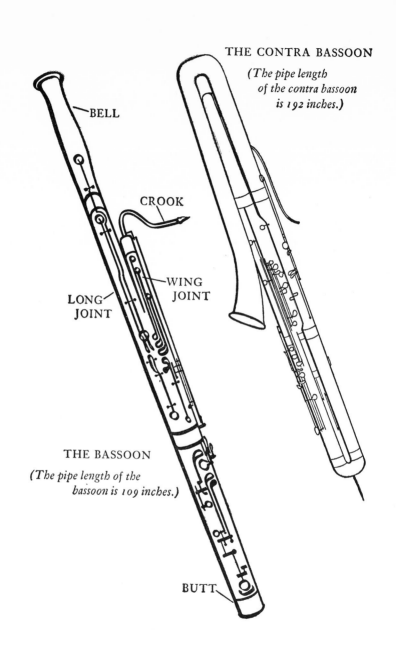

**THE CONTRA BASSOON**

*(The pipe length
of the contra bassoon
is 192 inches.)*

BELL

CROOK

WING
JOINT

LONG
JOINT

**THE BASSOON**

*(The pipe length of the
bassoon is 109 inches.)*

BUTT

# THE BASSOON

WILLIAM POLISI, first bassoonist of the New York Philharmonic-Symphony Orchestra, played for three years in
the Cleveland Orchestra and thereafter for six years in
the National Broadcasting Company Symphony Orchestra.
He took up his instrument because he wanted to play in
a symphony orchestra and knew he couldn't, just playing
the piano; and because his father, a tuba player, thought
it would be nice to have another bass player in the family.
For a while during the depression, although he was a grad-
uate of the Curtis Institute of Music in Philadelphia and
recognized as an expert bassoonist, he was out of a job, and
took up farming. He really likes his instrument—likes its
tone, likes to blow into it. He used to practice six hours
a day on it. Now he does not practice so much, but he has
a definite warming-up routine before concerts: (1) technical exercises; (2) sustained notes; (3) staccato passages.
He tends his reeds as a mother tends her babies, carries six
to ten of them around with him all the time for a quick
change when the music calls for pianissimo, staccato, high
register. In Beethoven's Fourth, for instance, he uses one
reed for the first three Movements, then, in the last, when
it comes to the famous staccato passage:

he changes to a very sharp staccato reed. He warms up the reeds by playing on them backstage before concerts. He says, "A reed can make you sound like a professional or an amateur." He speaks with great feeling of his teacher, J. Walter Guetter. He points out proudly that his name is on the Shostakovich Ninth Symphony recording as bassoon soloist. However, in the furthest flights of his imagination he never hopes to tour as soloist, quietly accepting the fact that a bassoonist cannot make a career as concert artist. "There are two standard concertos for bassoon," he says wistfully, "the Mozart and the Weber. When you are going to appear as soloist you just play one or the other."

The bassoon is held slanting across the player's left shoulder, chest, and right leg, with the left hand uppermost, at the level of the player's breast, and the right hand somewhat below and behind the right thigh. Its weight is supported largely by a strong cord which runs around the neck. The instrument has five parts: the crook (that slender tube into which the player blows); the wing joint (the part of the pipe that descends floorward); the butt (the wooden bottom part in the shape of a *U* where the pipe doubles back); the long joint (the part that ascends up past the player's shoulder and above his head); and the bell (the part from which emerges the music, lugubrious, serene, melancholy, or whimsical). Its air column would measure 109 inches stretched out, and, even doubled back on itself, the instrument is four feet long.

Since the bassoon is a double-reed instrument, like the oboe and the English horn, the sound is created by two halves of a reed in the mouthpiece vibrating against each other. The instrument, moreover, has a conical tube (the clarinet's is cylindrical) and overblows at the interval of an octave (the clarinet overblows at a twelfth), a factor which determines the mechanism of the upper-note range and also calls for a niceness in breath control, which only the most assiduous can obtain.

Its range is:

The notes above the top B-flat are, however, somewhat ineffective. A high E has been added to many instruments. The Ravel Piano Concerto calls for this E, and those lacking it have to "fake." This extended scale is made possible by variations in blowing, lipping, and fingering.

Bassoons in the symphony orchestra add sonority to the basses; enrich inner parts without themselves becoming conspicuous; blend their tones, as the bass of the wood winds, with oboes, horns, and clarinets. They serve to soften a tone that might otherwise be strident, bolster up a weak portion in the range of another instrument, add staccato impetus to low voicings. And at times they emerge in semi-solo passages.

To do all this the bassoonist has to possess much more than a cooperative sense. What with this instrument's uneven scale, its sensitivity to temperatures and its general moodiness, he has to exert unusual fortitude and persuasiveness. Moreover, since bassoons differ, one instrument from another, each player must become accustomed to his own particular instrument's peculiarities, learn to amplify weak notes in the scale, correct inherently faulty intonation.

The expert bassoonist must be something of an actor, too. He must augment the instrument's clowning propensities when the passage struts or cavorts. He must make it warmly persuasive as in the Third Movement of Tchaikovsky's Fifth Symphony. He must bring out the lyrical quality as in the Second Movement of Beethoven's Fifth, or in Grieg's "Allegretto Pastorale" from the *Peer Gynt Suite*.

Composers have used the bassoon to attain a wide variety of effects. Stravinsky chose it to introduce his most controversial work, *Le Sacre du printemps*, because with its eerie, unearthly upper register notes, it brings the attention to prickling alertness. Tchaikovsky set the mood of melancholy in his *Pathètique Symphony* by giving it the opening brooding passages.

Nor have composers neglected its capacity to be funny. Deems Taylor gave it leeway in this direction when he scored a passage for it in his *Looking-Glass Suite*. Dukas used it to display the sprawling, clownish antics of the broom in his *Sorcerer's Apprentice*. The instrument gets a laugh, perhaps, through its curious blending of ponderousness and agility, something like a fat man doing a cakewalk.

Of the three (sometimes four) bassoonists usually included in the symphony orchestra, one of them doubles on the contra bassoon. Most contra bassoonists begin as bassoonists and switch instruments later in life. They are in great demand, because of their scarcity and because a symphony orchestra needs one urgently for effects unattainable by any other instrument.

The contra bassoon, playing an octave lower than the bassoon, provides ponderousness, ominousness, and, at times, humor. When John the Baptist's head is severed in Strauss's *Salome*, we hear its rumbling tones deep down in the orchestra's depths. In the prison scene of *Fidelio*, the hollowness of the dungeon is brought home by a few of its subterranean notes. In Haydn's *Creation* when in the passage, "By heavy beasts the ground is trod," the last word is intoned, its low note is sounded fortissimo, producing an impression of unbearable weight.

Since depth of tone is contingent on length of pipe, it is not surprising to learn that the contra bassoon's pipe, if stretched out straight, would be sixteen feet long. Doubled back on itself and steadied at the floor end by means of a long peg, it is still almost as tall as a man. Unlike the bassoon, its bell points downward. This instrument requires of the player exceptional breath control.

A family of bassoonists whose influence is especially widespread is the Reines family. The father, Morris, played contra bassoon in the New York Philharmonic for eleven years. Five of his sons and two of his grandchildren have made careers as bassoonists. Of the sons, Leo Reines has played contra bassoon in the Cincinnati Symphony

Orchestra for thirty years; Abraham Reines has been bassoonist of the N.B.C. Symphony Orchestra for sixteen years; another brother has played in the Chicago and St. Louis symphonies, and still another in the New York Philharmonic. One of the grandsons plays in the Navy Band in Washington.

The bassoons trace back to a large family of instruments in the Middle Ages called bombards, pommers, or brummers. These were unwieldy instruments since no one had yet hit on the idea of doubling back the pipe—a device that, incidentally, made it possible for the fingers to control holes throughout the length of the instrument, and thus extend the scale.

Even as they are constructed today, the bassoon and the contra bassoon are capricious instruments. But all attempts that have been made to regulate and "set" their scale have seemed to diminish their flexibility in rapid passages or make their tone less distinctive.

So the bassoon continues on its path of human frailty. The sound still comes out as—bassoon sound. And players still like to blow into and finger the instrument, in spite of —or rather, because of—its flaws.

CHAPTER XIII  →»» *The Clarinet* «←

*It plays for symphony and swing,*
*Plays loud and soft and everything,*
*Its scale's as fluid as a river*
*And takes high notes without a quiver.*

THE BASS CLARINET

THE CLARINET

# THE CLARINET

THE bassoon, the harp, or the xylophone may be reserved for special effects. The tuba may wait a whole season for that one solo. The cymbals may prove their worth by the single stentorian crash. But the clarinet knows no such self-effacement, no such specialization. It is continually in service, is capable of practically all effects. It never misses a symphony, never goes unheard when playing. It is stormy, cool, sensuous, noble, ironic, serene, strident, luscious, chaste, and raucous. It is work horse and race horse, chariot and wheelbarrow, champagne and spinach. It is as modern as gyroscopes and as timeless as the seas. It is at home equally in symphony orchestras and in swing bands. It can produce almost any series of sounds: arpeggios, rapid passages, staccatos, legatos, fortes, and pianissimos. It is adjustable, versatile, companionable, indispensable. And it is very, very hard to play.

There are usually three or four clarinetists in major symphony orchestras. When there are four, two use B-flat; one, E-flat (the latter is a smaller instrument a perfect fourth above the clarinet in B-flat); and one, bass. (Smaller orchestras sometimes get along with two clarinetists on a permanent basis and hire the E-flat and bass clarinetists for the actual concerts.) But the story isn't told yet. There's the A clarinet, one half-tone lower than the

B-flat. This instrument is a stand-by for the two B-flat clarinetists. They use it when composers (1) want a somewhat deeper and fuller tone, and (2) when a passage is technically suited to it—"lies better under the fingers." So here we have the four clarinetists lined up: the two "firsts" playing either the B-flat or the A as need arises, the third playing primarily the E-flat, and the fourth playing the bass clarinet. Swing bands are another matter. We'll come to them later.

With the wood-wind instruments such a designation as B-flat, E-flat, or A does not mean the harmonic series, as it does, for instance, on the trumpet, but simply the scale most easily fingered on the instrument. It also indicates—since music for all "transposing instruments" is written in the key of C—the gap between the note heard and the note read on the written music. That is, if the player on the B-flat clarinet reads a C and presses what he calls a C key, the note sounded is B-flat. He is producing the B-flat scale without the trouble of having to read in flats.

Considering the versatility and the sheer application of modern composers in scoring for clarinet, it is strange to think that symphony orchestras ever got along without this instrument. But they did, and not so long ago, either. "If only we had clarinets!" moaned Mozart less than two hundred years ago. "You can't guess the lordly effect of a symphony with flutes, oboes and clarinets!" Luckily he did something besides moan about it. The clarinet, considered up to then an instrument fitted only for barn dancing and peasant weddings, became, under Mozart's sympathetic pen, one of the most respected and loved instruments in the symphony orchestra. His scoring for it brought out all its best points: witness his *Paris Symphony* as well as his twelve duos for clarinet and basset horn, his six trios for clarinets and bassoon, and his numerous other chamber arrangements. From Mozart on, two clarinets of the normal size were considered an indispensable feature of every symphony orchestra.

During this time, to keep pace with its growing prominence, the instrument itself was being improved. More keys were being added; the key mechanism was being perfected; the scale was getting more even; the instruments were becoming more regularized. It was not until 1825 to 1835, however, that the thirteen-keyed clarinet really established itself. The clarinet then reached a status in which uniformity of tone was the norm, and trills and legato passages could be executed with ease. Hyacinth Klosé, a professor at the Paris Conservatory, deserves much of the credit for stabilizing these improvements since in 1843 he completely reorganized the fingering of the instrument, adapting it to a system commonly known as the Boehm.

Not that the clarinet has ever reached the chilly state of utter perfection. The player still has to humor along some of the notes to get them in tune. The keys are apt to rattle, making it something of a trick to play solos softly. Then there are the throat notes (three or four in the middle register) that no amount of indulgence can make sound nice and round.

A word about the clarinet's mechanics: Unlike the oboe, the English horn, and the bassoon, in which the sound is created by two halves of a reed in the mouthpiece vibrating against each other, the clarinet is a single-reed instrument. This single reed vibrates against a slot in the mouthpiece. Next about the layout of the keys: Their pattern begins to repeat, not after an octave but after a twelfth. This arrangement, caused by the instrument's overblowing at a twelfth instead of an octave, puts the novice into the same confusion as figuring in English money does a person accustomed to the decimal system. It means that the fingers do not slide along with the scale pattern as they do, for instance, in the piano. It means, too, that there are those two or three notes—the notes just before the first twelfth—that need to be particularly humored.

Then, too, what with the curious fingering and the sensitivity of the reed pipe (it is to all intents and purposes a closed pipe!), no two clarinets seem to function exactly alike. The player must get used to his own particular clarinet through a process of feeling, sensing, and experimenting. When he finally makes each tone come out clear, he has all the satisfaction of knowing that he is probably the only person in the world who can attain to just that perfection on his own special instrument. He has the satisfaction, too, of knowing that the power of crescendo and diminuendo is more considerable in the clarinets than in any other wind instruments. Also that several variations of single tonguing allow for a wide variety in staccatos.

Now for the clarinet's tone. It is characteristically rich, warm, velvety. Up high it is scintillating and penetrating. In its middle register it is full and mellow. Its lower tones —well, think of a boat sounding out in a fog-bound harbor. Then there are the sounds—ironic, mocking, raucous, such as are given out, for instance, in the opening of Gershwin's *Rhapsody in Blue* and the sound, unbelievably poignant, as projected in Tchaikovsky's *Pathétique*. And there is the shrill, hair-raising sound that describes the death throes of Till Eulenspiegel at the finale of the Richard Strauss score.

Considering such versatility, it is understandable that composers, once Mozart had opened up the way, by no means fought shy of the instrument. Beethoven wrote three duets, a trio, and a quintet in which it figured prominently. Weber, another of its protagonists, wrote two concertos, and a concertino, as well as a very showy Grand Duo Concertante for Clarinet and Piano. Schubert's "Der Hirt auf dem Felsen" has a notable clarinet obbligato. Schumann wrote three fantasy pieces for clarinet and piano, and *Four Fairy Tales* for clarinet, viola, and piano. Mendelssohn wrote two concert pieces for clarinet, basset horn (a variant of the clarinet), and piano. Brahms wrote two sonatas, a trio, a quintet in which it figured.

A sonata came from the pen of Saint-Saëns, and, from Debussy, a rhapsody for clarinet and orchestra as well as a little piece for clarinet and piano. D'Indy, Poulenc, Honegger, Berg, Stravinsky, Dubensky, have all recognized its worth, as well as the American composers E. Burlingame Hill (Sonatina for Clarinet and Piano), Daniel Gregory Mason (Sonata for Clarinet and Piano, Duet for Clarinet and Piano, Trio for Clarinet, Violin, and Piano), and Roy Harris (Sextet for Clarinet, String Quartet, and Piano).

The E-flat clarinet was used as the underlying motif in

Berlioz' *Symphonie fantastique*. Parts for the E-flat clarinet are also found in Strauss's *Ein Heldenleben*, in Stravinsky's *Le Sacre du printemps*, and in Ravel's *Daphnis et Chloé*.

The clarinet's big brother, the bass clarinet, lies an octave below the range of the B-flat, but avoids an unwieldy length (the deeper the tone, the longer the pipe) by having its lower end curved upward ending in a bell and by having the upper end of the tube bent downward, so bringing the reed within reach of the player's mouth. It is always patterned in B-flat. For a time there were variations in the model but the clarinetists got tired of lugging around two of the heavy instruments, and saw to it that composers rescored their works for one standard bass. This sounds from:

and the tone quality though similar to the ordinary clarinets is also "looser" or more "hollow." It brought to Berlioz' mind—and he used it accordingly—"great churches with dim aisles filled with slowly moving processions chanting solemn music." Tchaikovsky wisely chose it, instead of the bassoon, in the first movement of his *Pathétique* for the four notes which he indicated to be played *pppppp* to make certain of the theme dying away into utter and exquisite nothingness.

To become conscious of the four stalwart manipulators of the clarinets in our symphony orchestras is, however, to know how only half of their world lives. One has still to realize that the clarinet takes the place of the violin in concert bands. As for swing bands—that's a story in itself.

It's a story of an instrument that moves with equal ease in symphonic and swing circles, its diversified individuality an asset to both. Just calling up the name of Benny Goodman—who plays with such aplomb Debussy's First Rhapsody for Clarinet and Orchestra and the latest swing hit; Mozart's Quintet for Clarinet and Strings and bobbysoxers' favorite dance tune; Bartók's *Contrasts for Violin, Clarinet, and Orchestra* and be-bop—is to make the erstwhile yawning gap between symphony and swing shrink to the imaginary line geometrists trace between any two given points.

The clarinet, in other words, crosses the hair line (long hair or short means little to it) without so much as a semi-quaver. In swing bands it is responsible for much of the melody. Its utterances are integral, and, to a degree surprising in jazz, logical. Of course it goes off into florid improvisations, too, and of course it relies on extra-musical "effects." But in rapid passages it is explicit. Its two tonal characteristics—upper register: clear, penetrating; lower register: sweet and "hot"—are more than useful. Besides its key system permits lightning execution. Finally, it is capable of that candid, ironic expression which is the basis of jazz. One might call it, in short, glue to the dispersive elements in any swing ensemble.

As for those "effects": there is the subtone, unknown in the symphony orchestra, but an everyday affair in jazz. This tone has the curious knack of being scarcely audible to the naked ear, yet, played at the microphone, becoming big as a house. And it sounds wonderful! Then there is the choir tone which Glenn Miller's orchestra developed —full, rich, florescent. Finally, there is that ironic blatting which may be said to be the source sound of all jazz.

But we leave an incorrect impression with this picture of clarinetists spending their days in the excitement of improvisation, the enthrallment of interpretation and the glow of success. As a matter of fact, they spend a good part of their days just tending their reeds. Robert McGinnis, first clarinetist of the New York Philharmonic-Symphony Orchestra, estimates that the average clarinetist spends from four to ten hours a week pruning, clipping, shaping, and otherwise preparing his reeds.

Remember, then, symphony or swing, loud or soft, flamboyant or subdued, those clarinets mean not only thrill and creativeness, but practically a whole day extra each week spent just in preparing the instrument for performance. So when next you hear Strauss's Till Eulenspiegel shrieking in his death throes, and the lover's sword clashing against the crackling flames in *Siegfried*, spare a thought for life's ironies as epitomized in the clarinet.

## CHAPTER XIV

# ⇒» The Oboe and the English Horn «⇐

Veiled, soft and sad the oboe's tone;
Not veiled or soft the player's groan.
On mornings when his reeds he whittles
He swears at life and shuns his victuals.
He wishes he had ne'er been born
Or learned oboe and English horn.

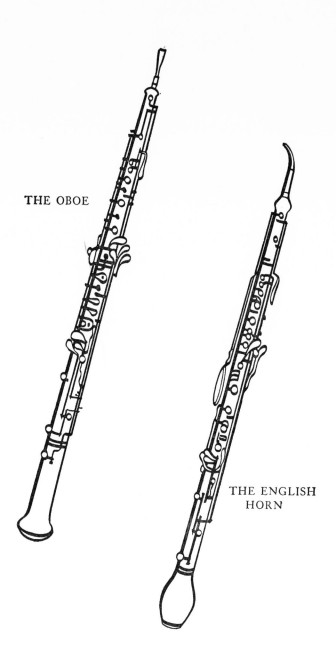

THE OBOE

THE ENGLISH
HORN

# THE OBOE AND THE
# ENGLISH HORN

THE oboist, like the student surgeon, may as well give up all hope of making the grade in his profession if he does not relish handling a knife. For oboe players—and I'm talking now of the skilled ones as well as of the amateurs —spend almost as much time whittling their reed mouth-pieces as they do practicing their scales. When I asked why some enterprising soul didn't set up as a reed-maker, the way shoemakers and watchmakers hang out their shingles, one oboist who confesses he is a slave to his reeds shook his head ruefully. It couldn't be done, he said. An oboist's reed is too individual a thing. It has to fit *his* lips, *his* embouchure. It has to be as much a part of his per-sonality as the way he moves his mouth in speaking. No one person, however skilled he is in the art of whittling down the delicate cane to vocal proportions, could pos-sibly satisfy anyone but himself. Besides this, reeds are stubborn. Some reeds don't come out right at all, for any amount of labor spent on them. Eight out of nine have to be discarded. Only the person whose music is dependent on the quality of the reed would have patience enough for the task. In short, nearly every other instrumentalist suc-ceeds by fashioning music. The oboist has to fashion reeds, too.

The oboe is a double-reed instrument and therein lies its peculiar tone quality. I referred to this matter when I interviewed William Arrowsmith, first oboist of the Metropolitan Opera Orchestra, and he showed me a reed he had just pared into shape. It was as clever a piece of workmanship as could be found in any wood carver's studio. What an oboist does, in this fashioning process, is bend the reed back on itself, then cut across the looped end, thus making two reeds. Then he forms a tip by scraping ever so delicately till exactly the right proportions are secured. He then blows down between the two reeds to set them in vibration.

Directions for the reed-whittling process sent out by a well-known manufacturer of instruments reads like a manual on wood carving: "The knife should be one with a straight edge, blade about one-half inch in width, two and one-half inches in length kept sharp on an oilstone. . . . The scraping should always be done toward the tip. . . . Should the high notes not respond, cut off a minute portion from the tip of the reed." The same manual gives the firm and pointed supplementary assurance: "It is a discarded notion that oboe players are apt to become unbalanced mentally." Asked about this latter rumor, one oboist shrugged resignedly, "You probably have to be out of your head before deciding to take it up in the first place," he said.

If ever there was a basis for the contention that oboists are apt to go off the deep end, it probably arose from the need for players on the all-but-unmanageable oboes of olden days to "wear leather collars strapped around their necks so as not to burst the blood vessels and use a brass button at the bottom of the reed, against which they jammed their lips." Even with such precautions, "they blew," according to the same account, "until they suffered abdominal hemorrhages."

When commiserations are offered, however, oboe players rise up as a man to champion their instrument. The fact that it runs the gamut of emotions—tragic, comic, tender, persuasive, dreamy, melancholy, gay, detached— is stressed. Composers choose it for its remote quality, aloof from human passions, reminiscent of breeze-swept hills and cool glades. "It brings a ray of hope in the midst of torment," said Berlioz.

Expressiveness on the instrument comes hard. It is not only that the reeds are difficult to fashion. Once made, there is the problem of setting them in motion satisfactorily. The oboe player has to husband his breath as though he were in a mine cave-in and were apportioned only one good lungful an hour. Little air can pass through the narrow slit between the reeds, but that little has to be of unvarying quantity. Even when he changes the air in his lungs, the player's breath column must remain constant. The way a violinist must change the direction of his bow without a ripple in the tone.

The oboist's nice regard for breath control is indicated in the tightness of his lips. When I tried out a reed an oboist had whittled to shape, I found I had to bring the corners of my lips toward the center, not allow them to spread out. The skin of the lower jaw had to be held flat, not bunched up. The lower jaw couldn't protrude. All this just to bring out one little squeak! What, then, must be required for the full tone!

Thus in symphonic works the merciful composer gives the oboe player plenty of rests. He is not used as a background instrument, for he can't stand the strain of constant oom-pahs. He's used for the short but expressive solos. A perfect passage—not too long and not too short and just suited to the oboe's capacity for serenity—appears in the Third Movement of Beethoven's *Pastoral Symphony:*

Berlioz made use of this over-the-hills quality in the "Pastoral Scene" from his *Symphonie fantastique.* Saint-Saëns in his *Danse macabre* has it represent the crowing of the cock. Mournfulness is another quality astute composers have detected and made good use of—for instance, Beethoven in the Second Movement of his *Eroica Symphony.* Then there's the oboe's ability to sound exotic—a byproduct of the double reed, which it has in common with the Oriental instruments of snake-charmers and street beggars of Bagdad.

Oboes were used more extensively in the ensembles of the eighteenth century than they are now. For instance, in the Handel Commemoration at Westminster Abbey in 1784, a much-talked-of musical event of its day, no fewer than twenty-six oboes were employed. From 1700 to 1750 members of bands in some parts of Europe were known as "Hoboisten," indicating that practically the entire band played this instrument.

The oboe is not a transposing instrument. Its range, both as it is written and as it sounds, is:

The present form and use of the oboe may be said to date from the time of Haydn and Mozart, though it took exact form as late as 1880. The Paris Conservatory model, the one employed today, was adopted in 1882. The key mechanism is as complicated as it is ingenious, but, as we must emphasize again, finger dexterity in the oboe never takes precedence over beauty of tone. The solo passage of simple, tender quality is the oboe's glory, and this requires the sensitive embouchure rather than the lightning fingers.

Oboes are used to give the pitch in symphony orchestras not because they are constant in this regard themselves, but rather because they are probably more subject to vagaries of pitch than any other instrument—this again due to reed construction as well as to problems of temperature and humidity. The rest of the orchestra defers to the oboe, keeping step, so to speak, with the one instrument that itself cannot adjust.

The English horn is an oboe in the alto range, that is, five tones lower than the regular oboe. It's a little longer than its higher relative, and therefore, to make holding posture comfortable, has a bent back mouthpiece. It also has a globular, pear-shaped bell which gives it its resonant tone. It was used by Mozart and Gluck, but only with Wagner became a regular member of the orchestra. There are three oboe players in each complete symphony orchestra, one of whom concentrates on the English horn. The English horn has a double reed, too, and much of its range:

laps over the oboe's. It is often used for nostalgic passages, when sorrowful resignation is indicated. So Dvořák used it in the Largo ("Goin' Home") of his *New World Symphony*.

Berlioz speaks of the English horn as having a "melancholy, dreamy, rather noble voice" and says it is better than any other instrument in "exciting regret, in reviving images and sentiments of the past." Like the oboe, it plays the pastoral role well. Schumann employed it thus in his *Manfred*, Wagner in his *Tannhäuser*.

Probably four English horn players out of five will cite as one of the most beautiful of passages that from Act III of Wagner's *Tristan und Isolde*:

Here is depicted the longing of the dying Tristan as he awaits the coming of Isolde's ship. It has been called one of the most expressive phrases of all musical literature.

We wonder that no writer, in discussing the oboe or the English horn, has dwelt on the beauty of the instrument itself: the rich wood, the intricate key system (an oboist has three or four ways of playing almost every semi-tone), and the delicate shaping of the bell.

Seeing the instrument, a work of art in itself, one is impressed again with the manner in which the arts inter-twine: An artist created this instrument of musicians, and the musician himself turns wood carver as he fashions, painstakingly and with both an eye and an ear for beauty, the tools of his profession.

## CHAPTER XV

# »» *The Flute and the Piccolo* ««

*Flutes are made of silver, platinum,*
*When you play soft you're apt to flat in 'em.*
*If really high you choose to go,*
*Shift over to the piccolo.*

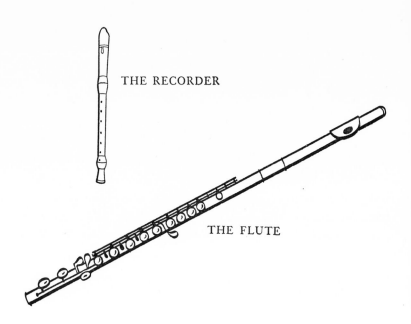

THE RECORDER

THE FLUTE

THE PICCOLO

# THE FLUTE AND THE PICCOLO

THE instruments in the wood-wind group come roughly in twos, and all except the flute-piccolo group have reeds. Deepest and least often used as solo instruments are the bassoon and contra bassoon. The clarinet and bass clarinet, versatile and vital, fill just about any role. Next higher in the scale are the oboe and English horn, with their remote yet comforting tone. And then come, highest of the wood-wind group, the flute and piccolo, with ranges:

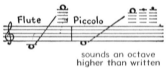

sounds an octave
higher than written

These last two can easily be spotted in orchestras, since they are the only wind instruments held sideways, that is, horizontally across the mouth. Moreover the flute and piccolo are the only instruments of this so-called "wood-wind" group which can respond to double-tonguing (*t-k-t-k*) and triple-tonguing (*t-t-k-t-t-k*). William Kincaid, dean of American flutists, explains that "embouchure, the manner in which the player uses the muscles of the lip, is the most important aspect of flute playing. Properly synchronized with sustained breath and fingering, it is everything in flute playing. Not that you can say to a beginner, 'You have a good embouchure or you haven't a good embouchure.' No. Embouchure is developed with practice."

The tone of the flute and piccolo is produced on the same principle used in blowing over the neck of an empty bottle; that is, the breath sets the column of air into vibration. In fact, air is all that does vibrate. It is this absence of reeds, strings, and membrane which gives the flute that singularly pure and detached tone. Change in pitch is effected by a shortening or lengthening of the air column, and this is done by stopping holes ranged along the instrument's length.

Hole-stopping used to be haphazard at best. The player just pressed the ball of the fingers on the holes. This made for so many inaccuracies that Rossini a century ago wisecracked, "Is there anything more distressing than the sound of a flute? . . . Yes, two of them played together."

All this was before the days of Theobold Boehm (1794-1881). This remarkable man, from the time he was sixteen to the day he died at eighty-eight, had one goal in life: to make a flute which was both accurate in pitch and controllable in tone. Apprenticed to a goldsmith in his early youth, he spent his evenings drawing tones of doubtful aesthetic value from the poor little affair that passed for a flute in his day. If it was pleasure for him, it was pain for his neighbors. In self-defense one of them, a professional flutist, offered to give him lessons. Within two years he had sufficiently proved his caliber to get a position in a theater orchestra. But by now his craftsman's mind had become more absorbed in the instrument than in his progress on it. Many notes of the scale couldn't be played at all, and those that did come out were notably off pitch. After taking two years of training at the University of Munich, learning principles of sound, he decided that tone holes without any mechanical stoppers were a liability. So he added keys that stopped the holes effectively and also, by an ingenious device of combination stopping, made all notes available even to quite short-fingered players. Next he turned his attention to the shape of the instrument and evolved from the conical affair then in vogue the cylindrical instrument we know today. In short, during the sixty or so years of his adult life, Boehm created an instrument "as precisely made as a first-class watch," one good for scalewise passages, arpeggios, grace notes, trills, rapid passages. Yet, for all the flute's efficiency, it is hampered by that bane of all instrumentalists—temperature. A slight out-of-tuneness may develop at extremes of heat or cold. There is also that almost human tendency to sharp in fortissimo passages and flat in pianissimo ones. We are glad for these small discrepancies. Perfection, after all, is apt to be dull.

As "coloratura soprano" of the wood winds, the flute is used oftenest by composers for a light, disembodied effect. For instance, the flutes portray the fairies' dance in Mendelssohn's *Midsummer Night's Dream:*

The faun that Debussy so delightfully sketches during a

half day's romp starts off its afternoon with a cascade of notes from the flute. However, Mr. Kincaid firmly maintains that his instrument is not confined to the portrayal of moods pixyish and ethereal. "Rightly produced," he explains, "the tones of the flute are capable of passionate utterance. Great composers have written passages of deep feeling for it." Brahms certainly meant it to sound so in the last movement of his First Symphony, for he designated forte appassionata the following passage for flute:

and in the Fourth Movement of his Fourth Symphony flutes give poignant expression to:

Mozart, in *The Magic Flute* chose this instrument to become the symbol of the hero's initiation into life's mysteries.

But its playful mood is perhaps the flute's chief attraction. Thus Ravel makes use of it in *La Flute enchantée* and Tchaikovsky in the "Dance of the Toy Flutes" from his *Nutcracker Suite*. And as for bird motifs, the flute has long since been accepted as the warbler of the orchestra, witness the *Pastoral Symphony* by Beethoven and *Peter and the Wolf* by Prokofiev.

There is at least one composition written especially for the platinum flute. However, since there are only six platinum flutes in the world, its sale to date has not been large.

It is *Density 21.5* by Edgar Varèse. The name, incidentally, refers to the molecular density of platinum, not to how some players feel when they attempt to play the work.

There are two or three flutes in every symphony orchestra. There is only one piccolo. Moreover, the piccolo is only half as long as the flute, rarely utilizes harmonics, and is, because of its smallness, hard to handle. Yet this undersized, scarcely two-octave, instrument stands out above all others whenever it gets even so much as a phrase to itself. No wonder Gluck in his *Iphigénie en Tauride* and Beethoven in his *Pastoral Symphony* used it for the portrayal of whistling winds and howling tempests. Berlioz in his *Damnation of Faust* had it suggest the infernal. And so it came to be called "the imp of the orchestra."

Among modern composers Shostakovich makes copious use of it, giving it a sustained solo passage in his Seventh Symphony, and Arcady Dubensky gave it solo prominence in his *Caprice*. Kleinsinger's *Pewee the Piccolo* was composed particularly to display the instrument. Sousa's *Stars and Stripes Forever* has a passage for piccolo which the great bandmaster pointed up for all it was worth. He had all his piccolo players march up to the footlights and play it with a mighty flourish. It always brought down the house. Piccolos in concert bands, besides doubling for the flute or clarinet an octave higher, take the part of the violin in the higher registers.

The problem of having a piccolo always available in major symphony orchestras is solved by having one flutist of the orchestra, "double" on the piccolo. (Flute players are always piccolo players and vice versa.) On rare occasions when two or even three piccolos are required, others of the flutes switch over. About half of the piccolo players use wooden instruments, conical in shape, and half, silver instruments, which may be either conical or cylindrical.

No matter which kind is being used, however, the instrument, curiously enough, sometimes sounds, even in the hands of the best players, slightly out of tune. Some authorities insist even that its being ever so little off pitch is exactly why it holds attention so effectively. The fact that in its low and more manageable register it goes often unheard might bear out this contention.

Numerous variants on the flute and piccolo are to be found in our orchestras and bands. The alto flute with the following range

but sounds a fourth lower

and a tone unusually dark and rich in the first two octaves is being heard with increasing frequency on light concert radio programs and in movie music backgrounds. Actually more than one hundred years old, this instrument is standard equipment for symphony orchestras and is employed by such serious composers as Ravel and Stravinsky.

Two species of flutes are holdovers from earlier days. The fife, side blown like the flute proper, with six to eight finger holes and usually no keys, was until recently the staple in "fife and drum corps."

Another of the flute's predecessors, the recorder, an

end-blown instrument with a "whistle" mouthpiece, has lately had a surprising re-emergence, especially as a home and school instrument. Few who play it, though, realize that it was one of the important instruments of the Renaissance, when it came in a wide variety of sizes and was seriously treated by composers. (Henry VIII possessed seventy-six recorders.) In the early eighteenth century J. S. Bach as well as most of his contemporaries called it *flauto* (flute), and designated the transverse type, (such as we have today) *traverso*, implying that the recorder was considered the standard flute of the day. However, after 1750 the instrument was little heard, was, in fact, lost to the world until in the early twentieth century chamber groups formed to revive old music began to include it in their instrumentation. Then manufacturers, impressed by the cheapness with which it could be made, the ease with which it could be learned, and the beauty of its tone, began to turn out recorders in all four ranges: soprano, alto, tenor, and bass. Those who choose it for their instrument today have at their disposal a great mass of music by the old masters, as well as numerous instruction books and compositions newly written for it.

## CHAPTER XVI

»» *The Saxophone* «‹

*The saxophone is sold in sizes,*
*It has more scope than one realizes;*
    *Its long cool moan,*
    *Its speaking tone*
*Should recommend the saxophone.*

# THE SAXOPHONE

In the late '20's the saxophone suddenly began to be conspicuous in dance bands. The cause of this sudden popularity is anybody's guess. It may have been because it is easy to "pick up." Or because it is flexible throughout its compass. Or because it comes in four ranges, like the human voice. Or it may have been its ability to sound deep like the bassoon, mellow like the cello, and bright like the flute; or its aptitude for curving around phrases and encompassing wide intervals; or, since it has characteristics of both the brass and the reed instruments, its ability to blend the tones of these two sections.

Or it may have been catapulted into public regard by the force of individuals: Rudy Wiedoeft's brilliant technique; Coleman Hawkins' new way of playing the tenor saxophone; the Brown brothers' richly interweaving harmonies; Jimmy Dorsey's free and easy delivery; the combination of Rudy Vallee's coaxing voice and persuasive sax. Anyway, the instrument came, was heard, and conquered. Those who had arrived at prom dance status by the early or mid twenties remember the thrill of first hearing and responding to that warm-sounding instrument with the curved neckpiece and the upturned bell.

The alto and tenor saxophones were heard most then, and are still heard most today. Those beautiful and flow-ing melodies that weave through dance numbers are usually played by the alto saxophone; but, when the blues set in, when you get "in the groove," the chances are the tenor saxes are taking over. Regulation dance band music is written now for five saxophones—two altos, two tenors, and a baritone—to balance the three trumpets and three trombones.

Dance bands which depend so much on the personalities and musical flair of their leaders are naturally subject to quick and dynamic changes. The concert band is a more stable unit. Fine blenders of brasses and reeds, saxophones have become "steadies" in these groups. Four are in ordinary use: two E-flat altos, one B-flat tenor, and one E-flat baritone, with less frequent additions of the B-flat bass (awkward to transport and hard to play) and the B-flat soprano. The latter high-pitched instrument is given a part in practically every full band score and is frequently heard in school bands.

The E-flat alto saxophones bolster up passages for weaker wood winds, bring them out without obscuring their essential character. The B-flat tenor similarly supports reeds and brasses in the tenor register. (Passages of cellolike quality are often given to the alto and tenor.) The E-flat baritone upholds the deeper register, one in which brasses and reeds in bands are traditionally weak. The B-flat bass tempers the brass tone of the tuba and mellows the bass in general. As a choir in the band, the saxophones give a special "color" provided by no other instruments.

But saxophones are not only rich and full in tone. They

have a composite range extraordinarily wide for wind instruments—that is, of five and a half octaves, from the lowest tone of the contrabass saxophone (this is not now on
the market, though a few are to be found) to the highest
tone of the E-flat sopranino saxophone.

This instrument of a multitude of uses is said to be
"easy." It is indeed easy to play the scale and simple tunes
presentably. But to gain mastery is another matter. For
one thing, its embouchure is quite different from that of
the clarinet. For another thing, double- and triple-tonguing are more difficult on this instrument than on the
brasses. Besides this, some trills come hard, though this
depends a great deal on the flexibility of the individual
player.

On the other hand, the fingering of the saxophone is
relatively easy, since it is laid out in octaves. (The clarinet is laid out in twelfths.) Like the piano, it goes along
with our harmonic system. Since you use exactly the same
fingers in sounding most octaves, such jumps as these

are easy to play. Moreover, the saxophone lends itself
easily to rapid scales, arpeggios, glissandos, and staccatos.

This most workable of instruments, combining the metal
tubing of a bugle, the mouthpiece and arrangement of
holes and keys of a clarinet, and the conical bore of an

oboe, was brought into being by Adolphe Sax. He began the eighty years of his existence in 1814 in Dinant, Belgium, and was practically brought up in his father's workshop where he daily imbibed the latter's enthusiasm for perfecting the flute and clarinet. Becoming a proficient player on both of these instruments, he in due course was enrolled in the Brussels Conservatory. From improving the mechanism of the clarinet, he went on to inventing an entirely new family of instruments. He made his way to Paris to market his inventions, set up shop in the Rue St. Georges in 1842. If his sole fortune at this time was his brains and his fingers—these and his persuasive personality—they proved ample. He gained influential friends. He displayed his invention in the French Exhibition of 1844 and won a silver medal. Later came gold medals and other honors (as well as a brief bout with bankruptcy), and his appointment as teacher of saxophone at the Paris Conservatory in 1857. A decided boost to his cause was the pitch reformation in 1859 which forced every orchestra and military band to get a new stock of instruments.

One of Sax's most loyal friends, Hector Berlioz, was also the earliest user of the instrument. He liked its "mellow, half-veiled" tone and he liked its versatility. He not only scored profusely for it but organized concerts featuring it. Writes Comettant of one of these concerts: "The last and most important passage was for the saxophone. A long-held note was conspicuously featured near the end of this solo. Sax played this note with great calm and assurance, swelling and diminishing the sound, giving it every nuance possible. He had forgot the fingering of the next note, and kept going in order to gain time. Finally his memory came back, just as his lungs were about exhausted. The passage ended, and the audience burst into enthusiastic applause: it appeared to the listeners that this very long holding of the note was proof of immense skill, and a bold and happy instrumental inspiration. The concert was a genuine triumph for the inventor."

Of such ingredients is success made!

Other composers have risen to champion the saxophone. Bizet in his Prelude to *L'Arlésienne* gives to the instrument a passage of surpassing beauty, the theme symbolizing "The Innocent":

Vaughan Williams in his *Job* ballet uses it to introduce Job's comforters. Ravel calls for the sopranino saxophone in his *Bolero*. Shostakovich in his polka from *The Golden Age* has a most effective passage for tenor saxophone:

D'Indy's *Fervaal* opera contains a quartet of saxophones, as does Richard Strauss's *Domestic Symphony*. And Carpenter's *Skyscrapers*, Hindemith's *Cardillac*, Holbrooke's *Apollo and the Seaman*, Werner Janssen's *New Year's Eve in New York*, Milhaud's *Scaramouche*, and Prokofiev's *Lieutenant Kije* all have important passages for saxophone.

Many works give the saxophone solo status. The "Concertino da Camera" for alto saxophone and orchestra, by Jacques Ibert is welcomed as an enrichment of saxophone literature. The saxophone is here given precedence over eleven instruments: flute, oboe, clarinet, bassoon, horn, trumpet, two violins, viola, cello, double bass. The number of instruments can be—and on occasion is—multiplied, making a concerto out of the work. In the composing of this concertino Mr. Ibert worked closely with Sigurd Rascher. Mr. Rascher has for almost twenty-five years pioneered for the saxophone, and a whole repertoire of works for the instrument has been composed especially for him. He has appeared with over a hundred of the world's great orchestras, among them the Boston Symphony and the New York Philharmonic-Symphony.

Paul Creston, who has written a Suite for Saxophone and Piano, a Sonata for Saxophone and Piano, and a Concerto for Saxophone and Orchestra, says that he chose so to feature the instrument because he likes its melodic quality, its dramatic capabilities, and the fact that it can maintain its own power. Another composer who is loud in its praise is Paul Hindemith. Of the alto saxophone he says, "It shows a balance of unhindered technique, expressive range and directness of speech that has its equal only in the modern flute."

The saxophonists' repertoire has been further enriched by Debussy's *Rhapsody for Saxophone and Orchestra*, and concertos by Eugene Bozza, Alexander Glazounov, Ralph Hermann, Lars Erik Larsson, Norman Demuth, and Josef Holbrooke. Vogel has to his credit, surprisingly, an oratorio with saxophones as the accompanying instrument. There is generous scoring for the instrument in the works of George Gershwin, Ferde Grofé and Arthur Shepherd.

When a saxophonist is required in a symphony orchestra, he is usually called in from outside, since no "regulars" are as a rule employed. Sometimes one or two of the clarinetists in an orchestra double on the saxophone. The Boston Symphony Orchestra finds its problems felicitously solved since three of the members of the violin section are also proficient on the saxophone.

So once again the saxophone maintains its position through its curiously adjustable nature. A sort of symbol, we'd say, of democracy—usable, comprehensible, convenient, available in emergencies—and human, too, in its strength and its weaknesses.

CHAPTER XVII  »» *The Bagpipe* ««

*The bagpipe is a nation's pride,*
*Not something one would care to hide;*
*So play it out beneath the skies,*
*Not by a crib for lullabies.*

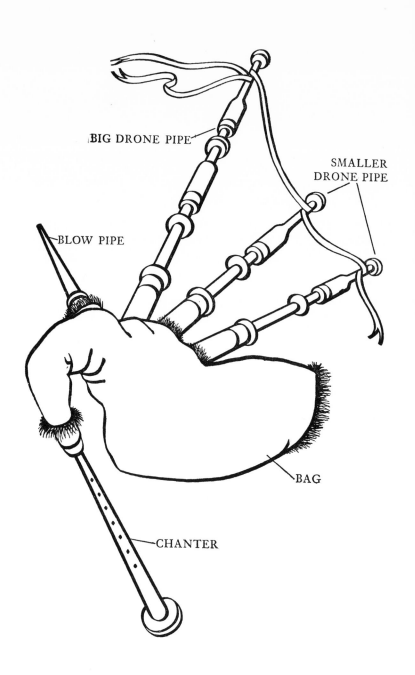

BIG DRONE PIPE

SMALLER
DRONE PIPE

BLOW PIPE

BAG

CHANTER

# THE BAGPIPE

THE bagpipe is a paradoxical instrument. It needs the open air, with preferably a few mountains thrown in, for a sounding board, yet it has but an innocent nine notes of range. It has no "harmony" yet it is the basis of an inexplicable (by the rules) aspect of harmony—the pedal point. Scottish regulations (Edinburgh competition, 1785) decree it shall be played in "the proper Highland habit"— the only instrument so set apart. Yet in the Middle Ages it was an instrument of beggars, hangers-on, ne'er-do-wells. It is blown by the mouth, but the mouth has nothing to do with the quality of its tone. It "talks" in a literal sense (take the word of the Scotch and the Irish) but its words cannot be translated into English. Finally, though the Scotch have taken it as their national instrument, they are frank in recognizing its limitations. They admit it is not suitable as chamber music; that it should not be played with a piano, to which it is not tuned; that it does not serve for lullabies; that it would be of doubtful value in the neurological wards of a hospital; that it cannot interpret "blues"; that it should never be practiced in a city apartment. At the same time they staunchly advocate its use for picnics, parades, open-air festivals, field-day events, pier and train farewells, and at-the-grave laments.

They will also proudly relate to you its distinguished history. Back in old Roman days, players on the simple pipes used to burst blood vessels trying to reach the far corners of the Colosseum. Sometimes two pipes were played by one player—one mouthpiece, that is, and two tubes. The resulting casualties impressed one player with the advisability of channeling or reserving the air so that the lungs could take an occasional rest.

The first bagpipe was just an elongated tube with an inflatable portion midway down its length. Later the bag was increased in size and held under the player's arm so that the elbow could deal out the air. Ancient Rome had these bagpipes. (On old coins you see its citizens, puffing away!) One hundred years before the Christian Era, Persia, Turkey, and Palestine knew them.

The Great Highland Bagpipe, the one seen in parades, has grown from this simple bag-plus-tube affair into a quite elaborate instrument.

The part blown into is called, reasonably enough, the blow pipe. It is a twelve-inch channel without side apertures and without reeds. It has one gadget, a valve at the far end, which prevents air from being sucked back and thus allows the player to breathe in as well as out.

The blow pipe sends air into the bag, a melon-shaped affair about twenty by nine inches, and made, in America at least, of elk's skin. For this one entrance there are four exits: a melody pipe called the chanter, and three single-note pipes called drones. The chanter has eight holes, seven in front for fingers and one at the top behind for the thumb. The notes sounded via these holes range from:

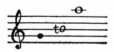

The chanter pipe—like the other pipes—is fitted into the bag by means of a "stock," a sort of base band, within which is the chanter's reed, shaped roughly like the reed of an oboe; two edges of cane tied together and vibrating against each other. The tone is also oboelike.

The three other exits, namely the drone pipes, have no side holes. They don't need them. Each sounds but a single note, and sounds that continuously so long as air is provided. The two shorter drones (each about twenty inches long) sound a note one octave below the chanter's lower A. The long drone (it's about three feet from bag to outlet) sounds an A one octave below *that*. The reeds of the drones are fashioned more on the clarinet order, that is, by splitting a round length of cane in such a way that the loose part vibrates like the "squeaker" a child forms from a blade of grass. The current of air issuing from the bag sets this loose part in vibration.

When deflated, the bag, with its three drone pipes, the chanter pipe, and the blow pipe, has almost an octopus look. But in playing position—big drone on left shoulder (some players use the right), smaller drones suspended by ribbons fan-wise from the long drone, bag under arm, elbow gently regulating air outlet, blow pipe to lips, chanter held in the fingers, player preferably walking back and forth briskly—it looks both efficient and imposing.

The chanter's eight holes allow for nine notes, counting the one sounded when all eight holes are stopped:

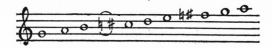

Because of the constant sounding of the drones' A's, the scale comes to our ears as the scale of A, with the initial G counted as a pre-note. However, it is an A-scale with a difference. It has (see illustration) an altered C-sharp and an altered F-sharp. These notes are neither sharps nor naturals, but tones sounding at a point midway between these. The bagpipe scale closely approximates the vocal scale of Damascus as sung in the middle of the nineteenth century, and some musicologists have decided from this that the bagpipe was imported into Europe during the Crusades.

If we hear bagpipes as discordant, that is because our ears are "set" to the piano scale. Note on the following chart of vibrations:

| | | | | | | | | |
|---|---|---|---|---|---|---|---|---|
| DAMASCUS VOCAL SCALE: | 441 | 495 | 540 | 587 | 661 | 721 | 786 | 882 |
| BAGPIPE: | 441 | 494 | 537 | 587 | 662 | 722 | 790 | 882 |
| PIANO: | 440 | 493.9 | ♮523.2 ♯554.4 | 587.3 | 659.2 | ♮698.4 ♯740.0 | ♮783 ♯830.6 | 880 |

that a discrepancy exists between bagpipe and piano scales not only in C and F but also in G. The bagpipe scale comes nearer to corresponding to the piano's G-natural than to the latter's G-sharp, which would ordinarily be sounded in the A-scale. This lowered seventh is what gives the bagpipe its almost Oriental flavor.

But more than the scale is different. The bagpipe, unlike the pipe organ or the accordion, has no shutting-off device.

Staccato notes or rests are impossible. One note leads on to the next. To avoid the dulling effect of constant legato, grace notes are introduced between melody notes. In "The Piper's Delight," a collection of bagpipe airs, at least half of all the notes are preceded by graces of one, two, three, or four notes each. Not a single rest sign occurs in the entire book.

With all this elaborate figuration, one would expect the bagpiper's fingers to be doing a jig all the time. They do, but not because the fingers have to stop many different holes. The grace notes are played not by multiple hole-stopping but by a maneuver of a single finger over a single hold. Such a grace as:

is formed, not by using the corresponding G-D-G-E pipe holes but by a certain method of lifting and replacing quickly a single finger on a single stop—"rolling" the finger, it is called.

This lavish use of grace notes, together with the uninterrupted flow of sound, the background of drones, and the piercing timbre of the longer-held notes, gives bagpipe music a curious resemblance to excited speech—to battle cries, exhortations, lamentations, incitations. Just as the human wail, its sob, its pleading, its complaining, is what we hear in saxophone music, so the heartier, more strident, martial inflections of the human voice are represented by the bagpipe. The scientist Baron von Kempelen, after long research, came to the conclusion that the music of the chanter reed was the nearest approach to the human voice to be found among musical instruments.

Early Celts were convinced of this fact. Pipe music, they maintained, was an actual language conveying messages with the explicitness of the spoken word—broadcasting warnings to distant friends, relaying battle declarations to foes miles away. One story goes that a bagpiper imprisoned in a castle beside the sea asked his captors, as a boat piloted by his kinsman, Collins, and filled with his brother clansmen, came into the bay, to be allowed to play from the castle parapet. This is what he "played":

> *Coll, O my dear, dinna come near,*
> *Dinna come near, dinna come near;*
> *Coll, O my dear, dinna come near,*
> *I'm prisoner here, I'm prisoner here.*

So of course the boat sailed on past. However, a piper in the enemy clan understood the pipe music, too, and the roof-top piper was therefore condemned to have his fingers cut off to prevent further impromptu broadcastings.

So thoroughly convinced were early Celts of the talkability of bagpipes, that, in training other pipers, they "spoke" the notes. Before a pupil was allowed a pipe in his hands, he was taught to chant words which stood, each, for a note with its grace note. "Hirrin," for instance, is three notes sounded by the little finger stopping a hole on the chanter in a special way. "Hinbandre" would be written, in our modern notation, so:

The nine notes of the chanter were represented by vowel sounds, in conjunction with certain consonants. Grace notes added consonants (sometimes vowels) to these sounds. Each syllable formed stood for a group of grace notes plus the main note. Syllables were joined to form words in much the same way that notes are tied in a staff. A familiar Scotch tune in syllabic "notation"—"I hin-do, ho-dro, hin-do, ho-dro, hin-do, ho-dro, hin-dra, ho-dra, hin-do, ho-dro, hin-da, chin-drine"—was so specific that pipers reading it in widely separated regions got the same tune from it. Thus music was handed down, at first orally, then in written syllables, from generation to generation. The Highlanders' wild martial tunes, called pibroch, were thus transmitted.

I would be writing this with my tongue in my cheek if I had not heard such syllable chanting by one of the few remaining pipers who understand the art—Patrick F. Meagher, of New York, erstwhile of Ireland. (Incidentally the Irish have quite as good a claim to the Highland bagpipe as the Scotch. It was played in Ireland probably before it was played in Scotland.) When Mr. Meagher played for me, "Yonder I Planted My Cabbages," then chanted it in syllables, I had an eerie sense of hearing the same thing twice and identically performed. I could not doubt that an expert piper, hearing the vocal sounds, could immediately reproduce them, grace notes and all, on the chanter.

This system of music transference is the more remarkable when one realizes that pipe bands—often with dozens of members—play in exact unison. All those hopping notes, those skirls and twists, are done simultaneously by all the members of a well-trained band. One can understand why a real piper must study for seven years to master his art.

Those bands, at least one of which is to be found in most of our larger cities, recruited, curiously enough, quite as often from Irish as from Scottish members of the community, consist of pipers and drummers in a ratio of about three to one. The bass drum sets the rhythm. The pipe major chooses the program, sets the general tempo, has charge of the band. There is no harmonizing. The bagpipes speak as one.

It's a brave sight and a brave sound they make. It's a sound we would not like to hear diminish in the corridors of time. For there is no sound like it on the face of the earth. And, given its peculiar method of production, there will probably be no sound developed like it ever again.

*Part 3*

→» PERCUSSION INSTRUMENTS «←

THE percussive section of a band or orchestra specializes in the spectacular and the explosive. Some of the percussive instruments have definite pitch, that is, play actual tones in the scale, notated on a staff, while some have indefinite pitch, that is, make sounds so split up into their component parts (overtones) that they cannot be placed at any one point on the staff, cannot be hummed or sung as single tones.

The distinctive aspect of any percussive instrument, however, is not its pitch (or lack of it) but its impact. Each percussive instrument, when sounded, has a decided effect on the time and tonal values of a composition. Pitched or unpitched, they bring out their sounds with such insistence and vehemence that they tend to dominate if not the harmonies at least the rhythms of the orchestra.

The word "percussive" means "the sharp striking of one object against another," but percussive effects among the various instruments are obtained not only by striking but also by clicking (as with castanets), by shaking (as with sleigh bells and tambourines), and by rubbing (as on the membranous portions of certain drums).

· 177 ·

## CHAPTER XVIII

# →» *Percussion Instruments* «←

*A rub-a-dub-dub,*
*A rub-a-dub-dub,*
*Three men beat a tub,*
*Beat a kettle, a skin,*
*Beat a triangle, tin,*
*Beat a cymbals, a gong,*
*Make the pipes go ding-dong;*
*In fact, there's no hushin'*
*Aggressive percussion.*

KETTLEDRUM

BASS DRUM

SNARE DRUM

TAMBOURINE

TRIANGLE

CYMBALS

GONG

GLOCKENSPIEL

XYLOPHONE

CHIMES

# PERCUSSION INSTRUMENTS

WHEN the cymbal player suddenly stands up, holds out two shining discs and lets go with a gigantic *wham*, then sits down and for the rest of the evening looks as though he were quietly working out a game of chess, don't decide, "That's a pipe job. Wish I could earn my living *that* way!" Because if you *were* a cymbal player and let your hands slip as easily into a false move as your mind slips into this false conclusion, you would keep your job just one week. The truth is, never was a profession more exacting. Never was a higher premium placed on poise, on control of the nerves, on split-second timing, on an inviolable sense of rhythm. One *wham* an evening perhaps. But if that wham comes one hairbreadth too late or too early, a concert is ruined, a reputation lost.

An inviolable sense of rhythm is but one of several absolute requirements of the percussionist. There is, for another, a highly developed sense of tone color. The true percussionist lives in a world of sound values and tonal shadings which the average person could scarcely even comprehend. Then, too, the true percussionist revels in dynamic power—in the burst of sound, in the enveloping thunder.

The very word "percussion" indicates the essential character of this section of the orchestra. Percussive instruments serve to bring the senses to focus, to startle, to arouse, even to incite. Thus parade bands, patriotic assemblies, political rallies are strong on percussion. Not that the percussive instruments cannot be charming, too. "The Dance of the Sugar-Plum Fairy" in Tchaikovsky's *Nutcracker Suite*, for instance, gets its quality of childish innocence and delight through use of the celesta. Percussive instruments can be lugubrious also—as witness the rattling bones (xylophone) in Saint-Saëns' *Danse macabre;* exotic, as is the triangle in Mozart's *Abduction from the Seraglio* or funereal as are the gongs sounding out in Gossec's *Marche funebre.*

In the smaller orchestras one man—and many folks consider watching him well worth the price of the ticket—leaps from cymbals to chimes, from triangle to gong. In orchestras of medium proportions there is usually a regular timpanist, plus a regular percussion man. The larger symphony orchestras have three or four members of the percussion section who, aside from the kettledrummer who "stays put," are able in moments of stress to give their attention to any of the large variety of instruments. It is to be understood, though, that each member is considered a specialist on one instrument, say, on the cymbals or the xylophone and, except in emergencies, reserves its use to himself. In many orchestras when the score calls for extra percussion, an extra man is engaged. When budget considerations make this impossible, as in the smaller orchestras, a note here and there just has to be skipped.

The whole percussion section includes—and we list them in alphabetical order, not in the order of frequency of use

—anvil, bass drum, castanets, celesta, chimes, Chinese drum, cymbals, glockenspiel, gong (tam-tam), kettle-drums, marimba, snare drum, tambourine, tenor drum, triangle, and xylophone. (We have given the piano, also percussive in its action, a chapter by itself.) Of course there are other percussive instruments used on occasion, witness the automobile honk in Gershwin's "An American in Paris" and the *sound* of an airplane propeller used in Antheil's *Ballet mécanique*. However, the foregoing list includes most of the instruments regularly struck, shaken, or rubbed to give rhythmic values to our symphony or-chestras and bands.

Probably because our age is one of starts and shocks, as well as one of inventiveness, modern scores are rich in per-cussive effects. These, in fact, are often bought ready-made. Unlike Beethoven, who created a storm in his *Pastoral Symphony* out of the usual orchestral ingredients, Grofé, in his *Grand Canyon Suite*, when he wants to simulate the sound of wind actually uses a wind machine. Ibert in his *Divertissement* indicates the whistling of a music hall audience by a siren. When Paul Hindemith, in his opera *Neues vom Tage* (News of the Day), wishes to give the effect of a typewriter tapping, he uses a type-writer. Respighi, in his *Pines of Rome*, duplicates the song of a nightingale by having the phonograph record of a nightingale's song actually sounded from the midst of the orchestra. The record, be it noted, is customarily "played" by one of the men in the percussion section. Also it is the percussion section that achieves, in Honegger's *Pacific 231*, the illusion of the sound of a train moving.

Percussion means *drums* to most people. Kettledrums (so named because they look like huge kettles covered with taut calfskin) dominate the section, whether they number two, as in some of the smaller orchestras, or three or even four, as in major symphony orchestras. Instruments of definite pitch, they have a composite range of about:

Kettledrums began to underline the key note of the scale and its fifth note even back in the seventeenth century, when they were used frequently with trumpets. Beethoven startled audiences by using them in octaves in his Eighth and Ninth symphonies, and Berlioz tuned them in thirds and fifths, thus making chordal effects possible.

Their pitch can be changed by hand or by a pedal device, and kettledrummers learn to become lightning quick at this, since changes often are required several times in the course of a single composition. Quick shifts in pitch are a requisite, for instance, in such works as Richard Strauss's "Salome's Dance," and in D'Indy's *Summer Day in the Mountains,* as well as in such modern American works as Copland's *Billy the Kid,* William Schuman's Third Symphony, Samuel Barber's First Symphony, and the latter's *Stop Watch and an Ordnance Map.*

The timpani (this is the other word for kettledrums) are used generally in forte passages to reinforce the wind instruments, especially the trumpets. The quality of their tone is determined by the kind of sticks used—ones encased in various thicknesses of wool or in hard felt, or plain wooden sticks with small knobbed heads—and by whether or not the drumheads themselves are muted or muffled by small pieces of cloth. Berlioz, in his *Symphonie fantastique* uses kettledrums (in chords) to represent distant thunder. Weber used their deep tremolo in *Der Freischütz* to indicate dark powers. Beethoven uses them to obtain, at the end if his Fourth Symphony, a mysterious pianissimo effect. And no one who has heard that thrilling and triumphant outburst in the scherzo of his Ninth Symphony can ever forget their sound.

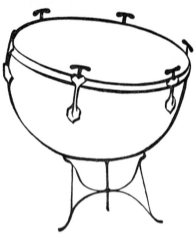

In modern compositions the kettledrums often actually carry the melody. Paul Hindemith's Concerto for Violin and Orchestra has a solo passage for timpani, and they play the one outstanding "tune" in William Schuman's Symphony No. 6.

Another versatile member of the drum family is the snare or side drum—that small cylindrical object with two heads (the "batter" head and the snare head) stretched

over a shell of metal. Gut or steel strings are extended over the snare-head side and it is their vibration which gives this drum its characteristic rattling sound. Thin hickory sticks are used to play it. It is body and bone to Ravel's *Bolero* and for that matter to most compositions in which the rhythm is pre-eminent. It is utilized most for its roll which produces a tremolo, for its "flam":

and for its "drag":

The tenor drum is larger than the snare drum and has a wooden shell deeper in relation to its diameter than that of the snare drum.

The bass drum, that largest member of the drum family —it measures from two to three feet in diameter—has thicker heads (stretched less tightly) than the two smaller drums. A soft-headed stick produces on it sounds thunderous or quietly awe-inspiring. Beethoven used it in the finale of his Ninth Symphony; Haydn scored it in his *Military Symphony;* Mozart used it in his *Il Seraglio,* and

Berlioz in his *Symphonie fantastique*. The bass drum supplies the steady boom, boom of the marching band.

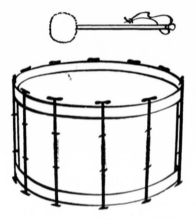

The Chinese drum, as its name implies, is used mostly to convey Oriental effects. The tone is hollow, dull, does not carry far.

Drums set the beat in the percussion section. The group that provides melody is called the "tuneful percussion." Most of these instruments possess bars which are graduated in size and arranged in scale progression like the keys of the piano.

The glockenspiel (this translates "bell-play") has a chromatic range that sounds:

though it is written:

The rectangular steel plates are arranged like a piano keyboard and are struck with hammers varying from wood to soft rubber. Composers use the glockenspiel sparingly since it has a tone as penetrating as an icy wind.

Through its employment, Wagner stepped up the "Dance of the Apprentices" (from *Die Meistersinger*) and Tchaikovsky gave the "Chinese Dance" in his *Nutcracker Suite* just the right lift.

The celesta is a sort of keyboard glockenspiel. In fact, it looks like a small upright piano, and it has a simplified piano action. Its tinkling, bell-like tone is put to excellent use in Tchaikovsky's *Nutcracker Suite* in the "Dance of the Sugar-Plum Fairy." He was probably the first composer to score for it. The instrument had just been invented and he ordered that it be delivered with the utmost secrecy to him in St. Petersburg lest Rimsky-Korsakov or Glazounov get wind of it first. The celesta is best adapted to arpeggios and light graceful chordal effects. Since its tones cannot be sustained any length of time, whatever melodies are assigned it contain no notes of great length. It also must be used with caution, since its tones are of an ethereal fragility.

Pitched an octave below the glockenspiel and considerably larger than it, the xylophone has bars of wood instead of steel, and a range of between three and four octaves. The player, a mallet in each hand, stands while perform-

ing. The tone is dry and wooden. That rattling of bones in Saint-Saëns' *Danse macabre* is the xylophone at its most characteristic.

The marimba, a variant of the xylophone, consists of a series of bars of wood cut to sound various notes, each bar equipped with a metal resonator tuned to it. Its resonators are longer than the xylophone's.

Of definite pitch also are the chimes, a set of metal tubes

—from eight to eighteen—suspended from a metal frame, tuned chromatically, and struck with a mallet. They simulate the sound of church bells admirably. Tchaikovsky uses them in his *1812 Overture*, Mahler in his Symphony

No. 2, Sibelius in the Fourth Movement of his Symphony No. 4, and Debussy in his *Iberia*.

Actual sleigh bells are used in Haydn's *Toy Symphony* and in Leroy Robertson's *Sleighbells*.

Most dramatic of instruments outside the realm of definite pitch are probably the cymbals, those two brass plates (with leather handles) made slightly convex so that the

edges will touch when they are struck together. There are five "effects" obtainable: a clashing together with a sideways movement; a single cymbal struck with a hard snare-drum stick or a soft timpani stick; a clashing together of two cymbals again and again as fast as possible; the performance on a single suspended cymbal of a roll with two hard snare-drum sticks or two soft timpani sticks; and the clashing of a free cymbal against one fastened to the shell of the bass drum, this last a maneuver which allows the drummer to sound his drum and cymbals simultaneously.

The gong (tam-tam) has a spine-shivering sound—low, brassy, crowded with overtones. Its immense circular disc is struck with a stick padded in several layers at the head. Even today China, Japan and Burma supply us with the

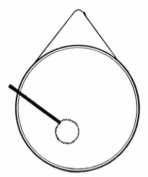

best of these instruments. Certainly the sound they convey is solemn, mysterious, fateful, like the East.

The tambourine, a small single-headed drum, in the shell of which are inserted "jingles," is played (1) by striking the head with the knuckles (the jingles are thus automatically set to sounding); (2) by shaking the whole shell, thus obtaining a "roll" of the jingles; or (3) by rubbing the thumb on the head, thus giving a tremolo to the jingles.

This instrument was used in almost its present form by the early Romans.

That small piece of steel bent in the shape of a triangle

—hence the name—and struck with a beater of the same material, was first used in Gluck's *Iphigénie en Tauride* and in Mozart's *Abduction from the Seraglio.* Liszt's Piano Concerto No. 1 in E-flat is often called "The Triangle Concerto," so lavish is his scoring for this instrument. Curiously, the triangle has the power of blending with whatever harmonies are played around it.

The anvil, an instrument of steel bars and a striker, is used, as one might guess, whenever the sound of an anvil is required, for instance, in Verdi's "Anvil Chorus" and in Wagner's *Das Rheingold.* This latter work calls for eighteen anvils, in three different sizes.

So here is the usual run of orchestral percussive instruments. They can be added to indefinitely since composers also score for castanets, rattle, guiro (a serrated gourd scraped with a stick—Prokofiev used it in *Alexander Nevsky*), chains, thunder machine, and any number of other sound gadgets modern inventiveness has thought up.

Varied as the instruments seem, proper execution on them requires qualities of character unvarying and dependable; in fact, utter precision, perfect sense of rhythm, muscular and nerve control, timbre awareness. Berlioz described the percussionist as "an excellent musician endowed with an ear of extreme delicacy." Incidentally Berlioz gave practical proof of his respect for the members of this section, since he used all of sixteen timpani with sixteen drummers beating them in his *Requiem.* It would have made him very happy, we are sure, could he have heard a modern percussion section executing Ravel's *Bolero,* Stravinsky's *L'Histoire du soldat* or Varèse's *Ionisation.*

*Part 4*

-»» KEYBOARD INSTRUMENTS «‹-

FOREWORD

"KEYBOARD" is an arbitrary designation based on outward appearance. We use it because it is a simple and a clear way of differentiating a certain group of instruments which otherwise would have to be corralled with strangely incongruous companions.

The piano, for instance, if one adheres to encyclopedic definitions, would be listed under "percussion," since the hammers strike the strings. The pipe organ would be classed as a wind instrument, as would the accordion. The carillon would be grouped under percussion, and the harpsichord under either strings or percussion.

The keyboard is simply a device for making playing easier, for which reason it has been resorted to in such modern instruments as the Theremin and the color organ.

The keys serve the same purpose as frets on the guitar, that is, to demarcate the tones. In most keyboard instruments, the octave pattern is discernible (white keys the diatonic scale, black keys the "sharps" and "flats"), with the C-major scale lying most easily under the hand in a central location. Horizontal keyboards have the "lower" tones on the left side and the "higher" tones on the right. In the accordion this keyboard is tilted up into a perpendicular position, thus bringing the "low" tones up toward the chin and the "high" tones down toward the feet. Just another of those paradoxes in the world of music.

CHAPTER XIX  →» *The Piano* «←

*Pianos by the millions sit*
*In homes at all points of the compass,*
*If they all played together, it*
*Would make considerable rumpus.*

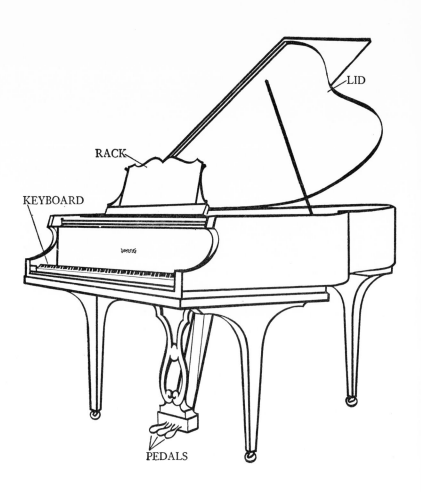

# THE PIANO

TALKING about the piano among the instruments is like talking about the earth in the planetary system. It is so much with us it is hard to view it from the outside. From 1813 to 1819 the Franklin warehouse in Baltimore turned out the then astonishing total of over fifty pianos. In 1939, in the month of November, 14,300 pianos were sold in the United States. For over a hundred years this instrument has dominated the home, the concert stage, and our harmonic system. For the piano is more than an instrument. It is the embodiment of our harmonic system.

If we look at the keyboard we see that the C major scale, which is a symbol of beginners' music (just as the *ABC*'s are a symbol of our written language) lies on the piano as that set of eight adjacent white keys, center, front—the most convenient and conspicuous place on the keyboard. Also, the sharps and flats are done up in black so as to be immediately recognizable. No such ready-to-eye-and-hand layout exists for nonkeyboard instruments. On the violin the player must hunt out scales as he would any other tonal progression. On wind instruments notes of the scales are curiously dispersed. But our harmonic system and the piano dovetail exactly—so exactly, in fact, that one wonders which caused which. Could it be that, because we finger our first music in scales on the piano, we think forever after in these particular scales? Could it be that the accessibility on the piano of the triad C-E-G has much to do with our harmonic viewpoint? In any case, the piano keyboard is so much ours that we feel toward it as we feel toward skyscrapers and well-paved roads. We cannot imagine a civilization without it. Yet when Colin McPhee in Bali invited natives to inspect the piano he had had shipped there, he found they could make neither head nor tail of it. Its key progressions, its chords, its whole- and half-tone spacings were without meaning to them.

The piano was tailored to fit our musical concept as it had developed back in the eighteenth century. Cristofori "invented" it about 1709, but many another ingenious craftsman had already been edging toward the finished product. Bach (1685-1750) helped along the process by making a tonal adjustment between the notes of each scale so that they could modulate one into another. Equal temperament, we call it. For instance, D-sharps were tuned down a little and E-flats tuned up a little until the two coincided in pitch. Modulation from one key to another was thus facilitated and those extra keys with which early keyboards were cluttered were eliminated. It was like spacing the rungs in a series of ladders so that a fireman might spring from one to another without changing levels. Improvements in the clavichord (the predecessor of the piano) were being sought. Hammers, strings, sounding boards were being tinkered with.

Cristofori called the piano at first *gravicembalo col piano e forte*—"harpsichord with soft and loud." At that stage he had done little more than introduce hammers to strike

the keys, rather than quills to pluck them as in the harpsichord. But this produced the essential quality that came
to be associated with the piano among keyboard instruments: the ability to play soft and loud and all the shadings in between. For a long while the piano was always
referred to—as it still is today by some precisionists—as
the pianoforte ("soft-loud").

There are 88 keys on the piano, covering seven and a
third octaves. There are, however, 245 strings. These are
made of steel; and, in the lower notes, they have a copper
or iron winding. This difference in number is only a seem-
ing shortage in keys, however. For, in the middle and
upper portions of the piano, each key causes the hammer
to strike three strings tuned in unison while five of the
keys in the lower part motivate two strings apiece.

The key, however, does not push the hammer against
the string directly. Four contrivances come into play:

   1. The key operates
   2. a trigger mechanism which sends the
   3. felt-covered hammers against
   4. a string.

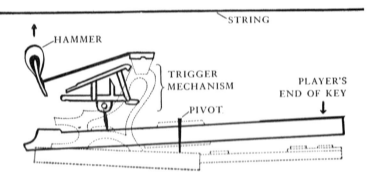

The hammer (through the aid of another mechanism) leaves the string the instant it strikes. A damper poised over the string or strings descends as the finger releases the key, shuts off the vibrations, causes the string to cease sounding the minute it is struck.

Ordinarily it does. But not when the right (or damper) pedal is used. This pedal holds the dampers off the strings (it is thus really an "un-damper" pedal), thus allowing all the strings sounded to vibrate freely. For its ability to blur the whole ensuing passage, this pedal becomes the novice's delight, for it blurs his mistakes as well. Good pianists use it advisedly—that is, only when the harmonies of the held-over notes do not conflict with subsequent tones.

The middle pedal, called the sustaining or sostenuto, is more discriminate. It sustains *only* the note or chord played just before it is pressed down. Even this effect is used with moderation by skilled pianists. It is a pedal for very special effects, and many pianos do not possess it at all. In the less expensive grade of pianos it is sometimes a "dummy." Sometimes, again, it is a muffler, for practice purposes only.

The soft pedal—the one at the left—so shifts the hammer that only one of the three (or two) strings that are allotted the key sounds. Fittingly enough, the sign for its use is *una corda*—"one string."

An ingenious space-saver in the mechanism of the piano is the "overstrung strings," the system of placing a portion of the strings in trellislike formation across and above the others. These can be seen when the lid is lifted at the back. This double tier of crisscrossed strings is attached to a metal framework capable of holding them at extreme tension.

Beneath the framework is the sounding board, a most important element in the piano's construction. However, it is not the wooden board itself that swells the sound. It is the air held encased between wood and strings. For this air, put in motion by the vibration of the strings, amplifies the sound and sweeps it out even over a vast concert hall.

This piano of a thousand effects and a thousand devices —what do modern pianists think of it? I put this question to ten of them: "In your mastery of the piano, what technical skill did you find it most difficult to acquire because of an inherent flaw in piano construction?" They one and all vociferously disclaimed the least discrepancy in their beloved instrument. However, I did extract a few hints of slight inconsistencies. They agree, for instance, that they have a common problem, that is, in achieving legato. The fact that the finger is powerless to do anything about the tone after it is struck "must remain," as one pianist put it, "a professional secret." The pianist must acquire a finger control which, through delicate spacing of notes, gives an illusion of sustained legato.

An even more searching criticism came from a pianist who makes annual nation-wide tours. It is that the concert or dance band pianist must contend with, not one piano, not even one touch or action, but with literally hundreds. An occasional virtuoso has his own piano— Paderewski's had a special kind of felt on the hammers— and his own piano tuner to accompany him on his travels, but most concert pianists must struggle along with whatever fare miscellaneous concert halls offer: the slow-actioned and the quick-actioned, pedals tight and loose, strings thick and thin. In short, pianists on tour must approach each new engagement with the resourcefulness of a jockey riding a different horse for every race.

Because it supplies both melody and accompaniment, both line and harmony, and because it is so easy to *play at*, the piano serves as the perfect writing desk for the composer. Sitting at its keyboard he can combine tones, test progressions, and weave harmonies, the miscellaneous sounds serving him as a kaleidoscope does the painter—to suggest other combinations and project him into new territories. Improvisation, composing extempore, is practically always a keyboard pursuit. After Haydn breakfasted, he spent an hour or so improvising at the piano. Mozart wrote to his father in 1781, "They are getting my room ready for me now. I am hurrying off to rent a clavier, for until there is one in my room I can't live in it. I have so much to compose and not a minute to lose."

After one of his long, rambling walks, Beethoven would rush to the piano, without stopping even to take off his hat, and work over his compositions. Wagner made the piano his working tool, consulting the keyboard again and again. He would play with his left hand, simultaneously jotting down notes with his right. He would try out complex chords with both hands until he got them right.

Inventive musicians, concerned with our "bondage" to the present modes, have attempted to widen horizons by changing the keyboard. Of course there were the mere positional changes: the Janko keyboard which simply rearranges the notes of the piano in six tiers something like the keys of a typewriter; the Mangeot keyboard which has two tiers, the lower (for the right hand) with the usual arrangement and the upper with the keys in reverse (high notes, left side); the Clutsam keyboard which catered to convenience by laying out the keys in an arc. More significant are the changes in tone relationships: the quarter-tone piano, for instance. This was first patented in 1892. Then in 1923 A. Foerster in Prague built a piano with two keyboards, the upper a quarter tone higher than the lower. Considerably encouraged by this invention, Alois Hába wrote the opera *The Mother* in quarter tones and it was given its first performance in 1931—without, however, world-sweeping repercussions. That year also Hans Barth patented a quarter-tone piano with two keyboards of eighty-eight notes each, the upper keyboard tuned to international pitch, the other a quarter tone lower.

Despite such experiments, the piano as it now stands seems in little danger of being superseded. Venturesome composers manage to go far afield even with the standard keyboard. Consider Henry Cowell's elbow work, Percy Grainger's fist thumping, and Charles Ives's directions for the playing of a passage from his Second Piano Sonata: "Play with 14¾-inch board long and heavy enough to press the keys down without striking." Scriabin in his piano music searched ceaselessly for new effects and qualities. Béla Bartók's *Mikrokosmos* is considered by Leichtentritt "a sort of dictionary of modern piano style . . . the student learns easily through ear and through fingers the complexities of modernistic polytonal harmony. . . ."

It would seem, in the face of this output by the most extreme of our modern composers, that the piano is a match for any amount of experimentation, that its horizons are limitless, that composers and pianists as yet unborn will find in its seven and a third octaves material enough to satisfy audiences as long as they have ears to hear and concert halls to congregate in.

CHAPTER XX  ⇢》 *The Pipe Organ* 《⇠

*An organ is a curious mixture,*
*Part music and part architecture.*
*Its structural significance*
*Leads to the fugue and not the dance.*

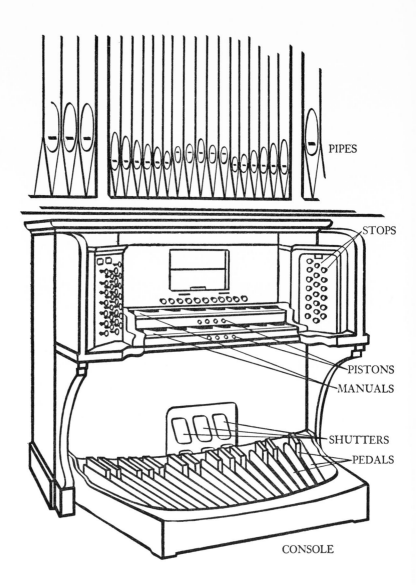

PIPES

STOPS

PISTONS

MANUALS

SHUTTERS

PEDALS

CONSOLE

# THE PIPE ORGAN

In a series describing the manipulation and function of various musical instruments, the pipe organ is often left out altogether. The reason for this omission is perhaps a feeling, not altogether unjustified, that the organ is not an instrument in the ordinary sense. With its four or so keyboards, its thousands of pipes,* its scores of tabs and knobs and pedals, its power to simulate a whole orchestra as well as each individual instrument, its space-filling propensities, and its monumental effects—all this weighed against the small figure at the console—one gets the idea that if an instrument is involved, man is the instrument. The pipe organ plays on him.

But in truth the organ is a wind instrument. The Scotch used to call it "a chest of whistles" and they were not far off. If it is also an integral part of the architecture of innumerable churches and concert halls, if it can outsound a waterfall, outweigh whole carloads of orchestras, and take months to build, it still makes music only because some human being, his hands and feet obeying impulses of his heart, can extract beauty from inanimate keys.

The organ started with Pan's pipes—a row of hollow

---

* The Carnegie Hall organ has 4381 pipes and stands five stories high. The organ in the Convention Hall, Atlantic City, is a seven-manual instrument with 1200 stops.

reeds bound together roughly to form a scale and sounded directly by the breath. Later a wind chest and bellows were added, and this continues today to be the basic principle of the organ. Of course little boys are no longer lured away from their swimming holes to pump organs of a Sunday morning, and organists don't come down with their fists on the keys as they had to on the unwieldy instruments of the Middle Ages. Now air is fanned into the organ's lungs by electric motors and the sound is released by the merest touch on the keyboard. An organ today actually consists of five separate organs: the great, the swell, the choir, the solo, and the pedal. Each has its separate keyboard; each has its separate function. Now, too, the shape, size, and material of which the pipes are made are infinitely varied to produce different kinds of tone. But, remember, the organ is still Pan's pipes, sounding with the same curiously unearthly sound, measureless and timeless, that echoed down the corridors of the dawn world.

A word about those five "organs" within a single pipe organ. The *great organ* has the more powerful stops to bring out the majesty and grandeur of the music. The *swell organ* is used for enriching the great organ with brilliancy of tone and color as well as dynamic shading. It has a number of diapason, flute, and string stops, a reed chorus topped by a mixture—compound overtones. The *choir organ* is used largely for accompanying, though it has some solo stops as well as harp and chimes. The *solo organ* has, as one might assume, more solo stops: flute, gamba, English horn, French horn, and the powerful "reeds"—trumpet, trombone, and tuba. The *pedal organ* functions in much the same way as the double bass and cello in the orchestra; that is, it provides the groundwork. One can play on two or more keyboards at once, sound two organs or even three or four through the medium of mechanical devices called couplers. Each organ chamber has its own separate shutter to control crescendo and decrescendo, and there is also a general crescendo pedal that controls the entire organ.

The hugeness and complexity of the modern organ make for complications. The touring organist can't carry his instrument in a case as can the violinist. A traveling pianist warms up on the platform piano in about ten minutes. The organist needs at least three hours to get acquainted with his instrument, since each pipe organ offers, according to its period, its make, its function, and the acoustical properties of its hall, endless variations and problems.

The end result of all this pother is to make the organist the most inveterate stay-at-homer of all instrumentalists. He is the church's organist as Rev. So-and-So is the church's minister. He is as integral a part of a moving picture theater as its frescoes. Bibliographies which allow Joachim to have been a violinist, and Paderewski to have been a pianist, immortalize Samuel Wesley as *organist of Camden Chapel*, Guilmant as *organist of Ste. Trinite*, and Widor as *organist of St. Sulpice*.

Sheer size stands in the way even of artistic worth in not a few of the pipe organs of modern manufacture. Two hands and two feet can do just so much, even if nimble wits guide them and a great soul motivates them. So the organist must hold in mind, against the temptation to become a cog in the machine, the fact that beyond all "effects" of which the instrument is capable—and these are almost limitless—lies that magnificent and unique tone which only an artist's untrammeled imagination can release.

And the technique for projecting this tone?

The organist requires first of all an exquisite sense of tone color and tonal balance. It is as if he had a roomful of palettes containing oils of every tint and depth; another roomful of chemicals for the manufacture of more colors; and a third roomful of brushes of every variety of texture and size with which to apply these tints. Yet, with all this wealth of color at hand, the painter in organ tones has aside from the very vague and general designations that composers old and new have seen fit to add to their scores, only his innate good taste to guide him. Each composition, therefore, far more than is the case with any other instrument, becomes a creation of the performer himself.

Then the organist must have a special touch, quite different from that, say, of the pianist. An organ key, once depressed, goes on sounding until it is released, and then just as suddenly stops sounding. The organist must be as precise as his instrument—press a note only exactly as long as he wants it to sound. He has to be able so to time this pressure and release in long passages that the intervals spell perfect legato. He has to be able to render absolute staccato when staccato is called for. Crispness of key touch (electro-pneumatic action on the organ has helped in this), a superlative sense of harmonic build-up and shading, and agility with hand and foot—these make the organist. Regarding the last requirement: the organist must be able to think *right hand, left hand, right foot, left foot* all at once and in terms of hundreds of stops, keys, and foot pedals *for every phrase*. Let the pianist or violinist ponder this fact.

But organists' virtuosity often goes unrecognized. It is because organ music comes so cheap. In churches organ music is thrown in free. The organist's role in the larger moving picture houses is taken for granted. The organist in department stores tucks in unobtrusively between rolls of yard goods. Organ music on radio is all too often just a filler-in.

Thus we have the curious contradiction of the player of this "king of instruments" often being reduced to wondering why he didn't take up the typewriter instead. But only in his weak moments. Let him sit at the console and bring into being the great works of the masters, release with one finger the sonorities of a whole orchestra, vibrate through great arched cathedrals, tear the planks off the very floor of the soul—then, despite the winds of ill fate and the rebuffs of his fellows, despite the dull routine and the scanty pay check, despite the (unpaid) summer recess and the unthinking public, he knows he has chosen well. He would not change his instrument for the most lucrative, facile, and portable tone box in the whole realm of music.

CHAPTER XXI »» *The Accordion* ««

*Music for mountain tops and ships,*
*Music you take with you on trips,*
*Music you dance to in the sun,*
*Music that's played for everyone—*
*Music of the accordion.*

BELLOWS

KEYBOARD

BUTTON BOARD

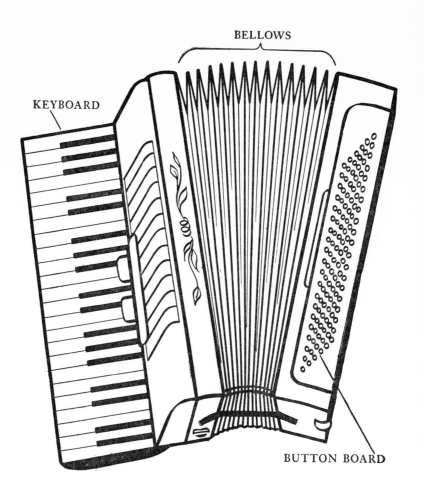

# THE ACCORDION

At a little hostelry halfway up the Gniesen in Switzer-
land they play the music of the accordion for the mountain
climbers. At a big party at New York's Waldorf-Astoria
to welcome a returning general the music provided was
music of the accordion. On a small freighter that chugs
across the Great Lakes, one of the deck hands plays the
accordion. Soldiers flying back from Bataan regretted that
they would be deprived of the accordion music they had
so enjoyed at the overseas canteens. They needn't have
worried. They had an accordion concert on the airplane
going home.

Accordions are played in schools, in night clubs, on
board ship, in lone forest huts, on ranches, in hospitals.
Associations of accordionists number thousands of members. In 1950 at least 150,000 accordions were sold in the
United States. What manner of instrument is this which,
like common people, God must love, since he allows so
many to exist?

Take a three-and-a-third-octave span of the piano keyboard, add bassoon, horn, organ, violin, oboe, clarinet, and
piccolo effects, sift in some deep bass chords, stir all with
a current of air, and you have an accordion. It plays in
chords—hence its name. Like the pipe organ and the parlor
organ but unlike most every other instrument, this "lap

organ" brings tones out in clusters. And these tones are not difficult to produce. By pressing down one finger on any button or key and drawing the bellows slowly in and out, the player can sound a great swelling mellifluous chord. It all comes from wind setting clustered reeds in motion.

Accordions come in a great number of sizes, named according to the number of chord combinations available, that is, the number of buttons on the board at the player's left: 12, 24, 32, 48, 60, 80, 90, 96, 99, 102, 111, 120, 123, 127, 140, 160 and 210 buttons. In the present chapter we are confining ourselves to the 120-bass standard accordion, that is, the type with 120 buttons on the board.

Suppose an accordion lies on the table with its works all spread out. The tuner is preparing to tune its reeds. (Professionals have their reeds tuned once a year at least.) In the standard accordion there are 448 reeds made of Swedish blue steel. It's up to this tuner to pare away these reeds, at the front in order to make them higher in tone, and at the back in order to make them lower in tone. When he puts them back into the accordion, he does not set one reed for one key or button as might be supposed, but places them in combinations, in chord clusters. In short, on the accordion the reeds are mechanically combined so that each touch of the finger produces a combination of tones. In the bass as many as eight tones are produced for one finger pressure. Naturally with all these mechanically placed chords there have to be duplicate reeds—many middle C's, many F's, each of which functions in a separate chord or octave combination. Another circumstance which sends up the number of reeds: an accordion uses one set of reeds for the bellows as they *expand* and an entirely different set as they *contract*—this so that it is possible to play any note at any time, regardless of the direction the bellows are taking.

The keys (those pianolike ivories under the right hand) play in chords of a sort—that is, in octaves. Depress any one key on the accordion keyboard and work the bellows, and you send wind scurrying over not one but *four* reeds. If the key depressed is the C above middle C, these reeds sound:

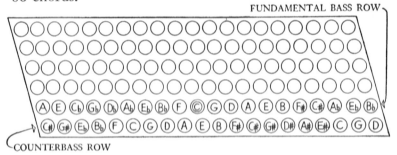

The button board of the standard 120-bass accordion is composed of 40 bass notes (sounded in octaves) and 80 chords.

FUNDAMENTAL BASS ROW

COUNTERBASS ROW

The two lettered rows play in octaves, the others in chords. The unlettered four rows use the same notes as the basis for their chords as the fundamental bass row uses.

When the buttons are pushed on the other four rows, the player gets those deep chords for which the accordion is famous. They are not chords formed by the player's own technique. They are chords built right into the works—chords prearranged by the inventor Damian of Vienna one hundred and more years ago—by him and later improvers.

Which chords did they fix into the works? First of all, the chord that appears in the bass of every hymn, every popular song, every classical number, every composition (barring the ultramodern) that our Western world has concocted—the simple major triad:

It is produced in any one of a variety of inversions whenever the player presses a button in the third row of the button board:

Note that only F, F-sharp, G, A-flat, and A have the one-three-five position of the chord. The reason for the up-side-downness of the other chords is that F on the fourth line of the bass clef is the lowest harmony note constructed in the reed set-up of the accordion. When a low note is lacking, therefore, the note an octave higher has to be substituted.

When a button is pressed in the fourth row, the player gets those somber minor chords beloved of gypsies, lone cowboys and blues singers:

Any button in the fifth row produces a dominant seventh chord. There will be one slight discrepancy, though. The chord's fifth step will be omitted, at least in the standard professional accordions. This is done for flexibility in modulating. Thus the C seventh plays C, E, and B-flat, omitting the G. If the fifth of the chord is really needed in the harmony, the player can supply it by pressing one of the buttons in the first two rows.

Finally, for those beautiful and vague diminished seventh chords, press any button in the sixth (outside) row. C diminished chord, for instance, plays C, A, and E-flat. The F button gives the following:

Note that here, too, a note is omitted.

Note also that on the button board each short row of buttons placed at an angle contains bass notes and chords related to one key.

Keyboard and button board are not the only sound-producing media of the accordion. In the modern standard accordion there are also "switches," one to sixteen tabs or buttons just above the keyboard. They function like stops on the old parlor organ, bring out new tone colors, such as bassoon, bandonion, horn, organ, musette, violin, oboe, clarinet, piccolo. They also make possible extremely high and extremely low tones, give the accordion a complete range of:

Finally, they divorce tones from their harmonies and bring them out in sharp relief.

Sharply outlined tones, however, are not the accordionist's greatest asset. He does best with full harmonies. He can sound like a whole orchestra and he can whisper like an aeolian harp. But he is at his best when chording.

To make the most of those harmonies, the bellows must be manipulated with the finesse of a violinist handling his bow. Like the violinist's up and down bow, they must be expanded and contracted evenly. At the turn from *out* to *in*, there can be only the breath of a pause. At this juncture the accordionist shows himself artisan or artist.

But he does not stop here. He has to have a harmonic sense as highly developed as the violinist's sense of pitch. String or wind players may study several years before becoming aware that two tones may sound well played together. Not so the accordionist. He must be chord conscious from the very first. Modulations must be his "meat." He must hear chords accompanying every melody. And he must be able to make transcriptions on sight.

Which brings us to the problem of notation.

A problem it is! There are in use today two ways of notating accordion music, each advocated by their respective adherents with all the ardor of a Dodgers-Giants line-up. The crux of the argument is the bass clef, since the treble is in both cases like the piano. The *single note* advocates want the bass part written in single notes with signs over them: "M" for the major chord row, "m" for the minor chord row, "7" for the dominant seventh chord

row, and "d" for the diminished seventh row—to indicate
the corresponding place on the button board:

The *full chord* advocates would have the bass chords
written out, as in piano music, with the corresponding
symbol placed above the chord:

Although formerly the written-out notation followed the
piano version (often unlike the accordion version with its
inverted chords), now the chords appear with the exact
sounds heard on the accordion, inversions and all.

Considering the sharpness of the notational controversy,
it speaks well for accordionists' ability to strike an even
keel that the International Confederation of Accordionists
at its Fifth World Congress, held January, 1950, in Paris,
agreed that "only time can finally settle this question."
Thus both notations continue to exist side by side—with
the student pretty much able to use whichever he prefers.

The professional arranger takes this situation in his stride
as he does his other difficulties. For instance, the accordionist cannot play long scales, arpeggios, or chromatic

progressions with ease. When these occur, the arranger seeks to substitute a rhythmic pattern in chords, such as:

(*From Richard Addinsell's "Warsaw Concerto" in Charles Nunzio's arrangement*)

Then, in order to retain the solo effect, the arranger often has to transfer basic runs in the piano's bass clef to the treble clef of the accordion:

(*From "Warsaw Concerto"*)

Finally, when the original composition is too high or too low for the accordion's range, the arranger must either invert the chord and supply the missing notes by writing in a bass note to be sounded via the first and second row accordion buttons, or use one of the switches which release high or low tones beyond the ordinary range of the accordion. This latter method necessarily changes the timbre, and he must take this into account.

Once he has adjusted to these contingencies, however, the arranger finds that piano, organ, violin, and orchestra literature lend themselves admirably to the accordion.

Literature written especially for the instrument bears serious study, too. Tchaikovsky and Prokofiev have scored for accordion in symphonic compositions. Roy Harris and Henry Cowell have written solo works for it, as have Galla-Rini and Virgil Thomson. In fact, it is possible to present quite dignified programs made up entirely of original accordion compositions. Still the original literature is comparatively limited. A regrettable situation.

Epecially regrettable it is when one considers the instrument's constantly growing popularity. The accordion is now heard in the nation's major concert halls. In Carnegie Hall, New York, in February, 1952, Sergei Matusewitch played a program made up of works of Bach, Mozart, Chopin, Mendelssohn, Frosini, Enesco, Granados, Rossini, Liszt, Tchaikovsky, Gliere and Sarasate. Moreover the accordion has been played as solo instrument with various symphony orchestras both in America and abroad. Besides, there are frequent appearances in private homes and clubs. Radio and television have given it especially gratifying boosts, since it is the ideal one-man orchestra and a visually satisfying one at that. Certainly an instrument of such gaiety, such heartiness, such good spirit, and such universality should have characteristic compositions written for it by great composers.

Not that those happy picnickers, those dancers on moonlight yachts, those guests at wedding banquets, those street throngs at a fiesta, those soldiers in canteens and hospitals give a thought to this. They know only that for them this is the instrument after their own hearts, the instrument they can have endless fun with, the instrument that never lets them down.

*Quills, couplers, racks,*

*Strings, nibs, and jacks—*

*That's what harpsichords are made of!*

*Thud, rustle, hum,*

*Neat measured strum—*

*That's what harpsichords are played of.*

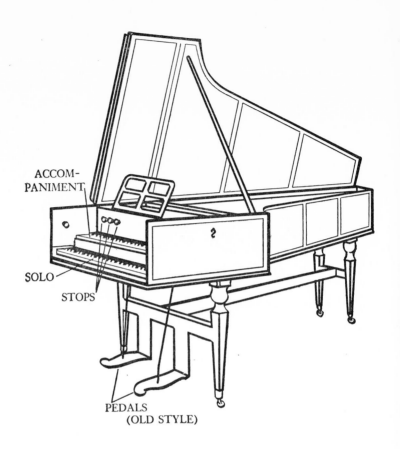

ACCOM-
PANIMENT

SOLO

STOPS

PEDALS
(OLD STYLE)

# THE HARPSICHORD

EVEN more than great paintings, even more than immortal musical compositions or great poems, musical instruments express their age. They have to express their age, because if they do not they cease to exist. The violin, the flute, the tuba are with us today—with us in our living orchestras, that is, not under glass cases in museums—because in their construction, in their range, in their tone and playability they meet the needs of this age. The bombardo, the tromba marina, the lyre, the ox horn, Pan's pipes are not with us because they do not meet our needs. How dead these latter are we do not like to think, knowing how once they must have stirred hearts and brightened faces.

The word "death" has not seemed so final, however, since we went to a harpsichord concert in Town Hall, New York. In fact, we ended up by wondering if, in the instance of this musical instrument, at least, death cannot be said to be conquered.

For the harpsichord which was consigned to oblivion throughout the nineteenth century is today being taught in many of our great music schools, is having music written for it by our great composers, is being played as a solo instrument with our major symphony orchestras, is being constructed by at least four prominent houses in Europe and America.

The reasons for its death and resurrection are worth looking into. This long, lean instrument with one straight side to accommodate the deeper strings ruled supreme among keyboard instruments in the sixteenth, seventeenth, and eighteenth centuries. Orchestras in those days—we can view them still (as they were represented by painters) idealized as angelic ensembles—practically always included a harpsichord or related keyboard instrument. The written music often showed only the main chords (figured bass) and the vocal part. The string- and wind-instrument players, twenty to forty of them, grouped themselves around the harpsichordist who improvised much as the pianist does today in jazz ensembles. The harpsichordist "chorded," motioned with his hands for one player to bring out a line, another to be sparing of ornamentation, still another to take over the theme. In fact, he provided unity for the group.

The harpsichord was indispensable to more formalized works, too. Oratorios as well as concerti grossi had each a harpsichordist serving as conductor, with usually another serving as accompanist.

Harpsichordists were an invariable adjunct of great houses. Johann Goldberg (Bach's *Goldberg Variations* were written for him), as harpsichordist for Count Kaiserling, had to move into the bedroom adjoining his master (who suffered from insomnia) in order to play for him during sleepless intervals—a sort of human bedside radio set. Since the *Goldberg Variations* are immensely difficult, this harpsichordist must have had unusual skill as well as unusual patience.

Harpsichord tuning was an established profession in London. All gentlemen of means had a regular tuner making weekly calls. Requilling was a frequent necessity, too. In America, Francis Hopkinson (1737-1791) not only helped write the Declaration of Independence but introduced a new method of tuning and changing the quills of the harpsichord.

Not a composer of the day but was saturated with the instrument's tone and technique. Mozart was brought up on it, wrote a concerto for it when he was around four, toured Europe and England in 1762 as a prodigy on it. Many of Beethoven's title pages read "for harpsichord or pianoforte." (This was true of "The Moonlight Sonata.") Haydn's Concerto in D for keyboard instrument and orchestra was undoubtedly written for harpsichord. Those prolific composers Purcell, Scarlatti, Couperin, Rameau, Bach, and Handel wrote reams for the instrument. It has more music originally written for it than has even the piano.

Supreme as it was, the harpsichord had its competitors. In London for a short time in the eighteenth century guitars took on a sudden popularity. Harpsichord makers breathed easier when a salesman with a new slant sold any number of cheap guitars to kitchen maids and street singers —making ladies "ashamed of their frivolous and vulgar taste" and sending them back to their harpsichords.

Then early in the eighteenth century came the piano, in the guise of an improved harpsichord, in a case exactly like the harpsichord's, under the name of "harpsichord with soft and loud." So alike in superficial characteristics were the two instruments that players on the pianoforte must have thought they were merely using a slightly different version of the harpsichord. But these early pianos were faulty and undependable. Not until the end of the eighteenth century did they, in improved form, begin to supersede the harpsichord. The last record of the use of the harpsichord in public, at least in Great Britain, was of its being played at the "King's Birthday Ode" at St. James' Palace in 1795.

After that the harpsichord's decline was precipitous and sure. Moscheles, coming to England in 1821, was unable to find a single harpsichord in London in first-rate playing condition. The whole of the nineteenth century passed without the Western world lifting, so to speak, the lid of a single harpsichord for any purpose other than to admire the paintings and carvings inside.

Then around 1920 the harpsichord began to be played and heard again, played by pianists who wanted to know how works by the old masters were really meant to sound (they got all the thrill one gets from restoring old paintings); heard by scholars who had read about the instrument's three-century supremacy and wanted to gain an insight into that period; sought out by music lovers who just liked its sound. Wanda Landowska, piano teacher at the Schola Cantorum in Paris from 1900 to 1913, perfected herself on the instrument. In 1913 she was called to Berlin as professor of the newly established harpsichord class at the conservatory there. After 1919 she directed harpsichord courses in Basel, London, and Fontainebleau. America heard her from 1923 on. She has confined her recitals

to works of the sixteenth-, seventeenth-, and eighteenth-
century composers.

Another protagonist of the harpsichord, Fernando
Valenti, who teaches the instrument at the Juilliard School
of Music in New York, believes that if it is to survive it
must be adapted to our modern cultural forms. He is
moreover doing something to bring this about. As harpsichordist he has recorded a movie sound track; has appeared
in television; has played in the New York production of
*The Enchanted*, Giraudoux' comedy with music by
Poulenc. This is the first time in modern theatrical history
that this instrument has been utilized in a legitimate production. This, Valenti believes, is the greatest opportunity
he has had to adapt his instrument to a popular idiom.

Sylvia Marlowe has introduced through her broadcasting programs over the N.B.C. and A.B.C. networks a
whole repertoire of contemporary works by de Falla,
Poulenc, Florent Schmitt, Vittorio Rieti, Richard Arnell,
Jerome Moross, Frank Martin, and Arthur Berger.

Such services of human intermediaries are necessary if
an instrument is to gain and hold its place. But these ef-
forts would be no more than a tilting at windmills if something in the instrument itself did not justify them.

Let's look, then, at the instrument.

The harpsichord is strung something like a grand piano
—though less tensely. The strings run (in three tiers one
on top of the other) away from the player and at right
angles to the keyboards. The whole layout of strings sug-
gests vaguely the harp. Like the harp, too, the strings are
plucked, not struck as in the piano and clavichord. The

plucking is done not directly by the finger, however, but by the finger depressing the key which

1. raises, see-saw fashion, a stilt (jack) from which
2. projects a small thorn of hard leather (formerly a crow quill) which
3. plucks the string as the jack flies up and past it.

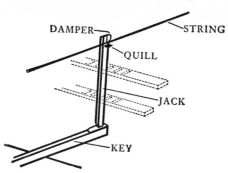

Another mechanism sends the jack back in such a way that the leather thorn avoids touching the string. When at rest the top of the jack lies a trifle below the string. Note that a string plucked in this way is outside the control of the finger of the player except to sound it. In other words, the harpsichordist cannot induce loud or soft through touch.

The keys of the harpsichord are laid out in two keyboards with five octaves each, the lower used generally for solo, the upper for accompaniment. The scope of these keyboards is extended both in range and in color by seven pedals clustered in arc-like formation near the player's feet. These used to be worked by hand as stops set above the keyboards. *If no pedal is depressed, the fingers fall on silent keys.*

The seven pedals (we describe here a Pleyel instrument such as Wanda Landowska uses) act on the tone as follows: the first (counting from the left) plays an octave lower than the key depressed by the finger; the second pedal gives audibility to the key depressed; the third pedal sounds the octave higher; the fourth couples the keyboards (makes them play as one); the fifth sounds pizzicato; the sixth gives a lute timbre; the seventh gives a dampened lute timbre. The first four pedals motivate the lower keyboard, the last three the upper. It is possible to lock the pedals (like certain keys on a typewriter) so that their effect continues without further foot ado. Thus three or four or even all seven pedals may be doing their work at the same time. Also any combination of pedals may be played. Thus, far from being a pair of keyboards of but five octaves, the harpsichord is a whole kaleidoscope of effects throughout seven octaves. For instance, a single finger can cause three notes to sound simultaneously; one manual can produce loud tones, while the other is sounding softly; lute sounds can be interwoven with harpsichord sounds; a shimmer of octaves can be made to accompany the single clear line; a coupling of the two keyboards can procure a crescendo effect. The combinations, in short, are practically endless.

Yet with this wealth of effects, the tone itself remains extraordinarily precise, neat, "a sort of thud plus a rustle." Since the tone starts to sound the instant the key is depressed and continues to vibrate delicately until the finger releases the key, the finger fall and rise must be exactly timed. This very nakedness of tone makes possible subtle and varied rhythms. Minute variations on the steady beat, the sudden cutting off of a note, the delayed action on it, all these serve to accentuate a phrase or note quite as effectively as hitting it harder. Besides, unlike the hitting method, the accentuation does not run the danger of hindering the flow of line.

Since complex rhythms, sinewy articulation, lean tracery are this age's special concern, the harpsichord's pungent performance, its pithy articulation have drawn many composers to it. Many of them have written seriously for the harpsichord in the past twenty-five years. In this, its affinity with the present age, lies the secret of its re-emergence. And in its nature, too, lies the reason why it was so conveniently forgotten through a whole century of emotionalism and overblown dynamics.

That the harpsichord ably takes on the task of interpreting this age is demonstrated afresh whenever it is used in jazz. It projects boogie-woogie to bring down the house. Tone clusters, clean line, ornamentation (effects), improvisations, dissonance, rhythmic figuration—they are all there, brought into play with a pungency only the harpsichord can boast.

What are the instrument's chances of surviving this, its second, birth? They are at least fair. Because not only art but science is on its side now. Harpsichords, which have been built in recent years by Dolmetsch, Pleyel, Neupert, Challis, have benefited from modern scientific knowledge and the greater availability of materials. Substitution of foot pedals for hand stops frees the hands for the keywork. Some modern makers construct the pedals with a half pitch, thus allowing the rack of jacks to be brought on only half the full distance, with the result that the leather tibs give the string a feebler pluck, enabling some gradation in dynamics. The strings of the modern harpsichord, more suitable in texture and set in a stronger framework, stay in tune better. A manufacturer in Detroit takes advantage of aluminum and of plastics, turning out instruments of immaculate precision and greater endurance.

The possibilities of the instrument in television are wide, for it is visually satisfying. Also it is an excellent accompanist for any chamber combination of old or new instruments.

But there are certain drawbacks which still baffle both science and art. A concert harpsichordist taking his instrument on tour (as he must) finds its delicate mechanism ill adjusted to the joggling of train and truck. Miss Marlowe, for instance, must turn mechanic before each concert, adjust a jack here, a pedal there. And, artist or no, one must take into account the tremendous expense involved in this freightage. Since the instrument itself costs from three thousand to seven thousand dollars, it is clear that only a mighty passion for it can induce one to consider it in professional terms.

Also (like foreign makes of automobiles) spare parts are hard to come by; the tuning expenses (the instrument must be tuned before every public appearance) are considerable; the instrument, too, is extremely susceptible to weather conditions.

However, where the end is worth the struggle, science and art together can work wonders. The harpsichord may not dominate the twentieth nor yet the twenty-first century; but it takes no special gift of prophecy to predict that it will be present in both, contributing line and rigor, serenity and sense to ages searching through what convolutions for the one straight course.

CHAPTER XXIII &raquo;&raquo;&raquo; *The Carillon* &laquo;&laquo;&laquo;

*No ticket office gateway bars*
*This concert hall among the stars.*

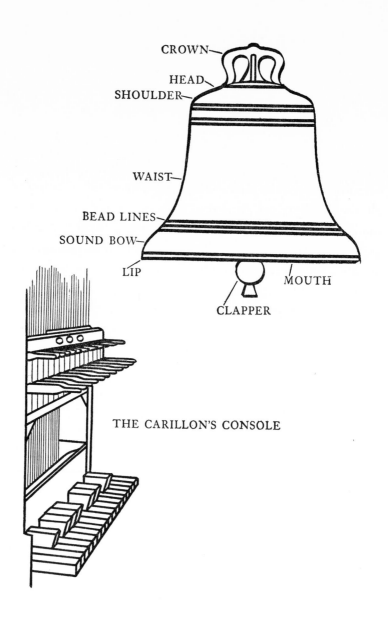

CROWN

HEAD

SHOULDER

WAIST

BEAD LINES

SOUND BOW

LIP

MOUTH

CLAPPER

THE CARILLON'S CONSOLE

# THE CARILLON

When the Freedom Bell was broadcast from Berlin in October, 1950, the sound was followed by the playing of all the carillons in America—seventy of them—sounding out a peal for unity and understanding among races and peoples. This is only one of many instances of bells giving significance to human happenings: peace proclamations, harvest ceremonies, Easter celebrations, declarations of independence, and that music—of which there is no equal—of bells all around the earth ringing out the Old Year with its faded hopes and ringing in the New Year with its infinite promise.

As democratic as dust, bells are used to serve man's daily needs: to announce a fire and call the housewife to the door, to start workers off to their jobs, to spread the news that a world champion has bitten the dust, to accompany farmer Sawyer driving his sleigh to market, to signal when the typist has reached the end of another line, to give notice that the Eskimo pie man is coming down the street, and to foment the countryside to quick action. Bells start the races, designate that Mr. Citizen has taken his stub at the cafeteria, mark sales on the cash register.

Bells' manipulation? They're played by clappers and by hammers, by little balls jiggling around inside a metal container and by electrical amplifiers, by men sitting snugly at keyboards and by men hanging lustily onto rope ends, by wooden barrels with pegs in them (after the manner of player piano rolls) and by delicately gloved fingers pressing the button on doorposts, by bell wethers gruesomely leading their flocks to slaughter and by ocean waves heaving against a buoy, by winds fanning brittle strands of glass on temple roofs and by cows swaying their clapper-hung necks over moist meadows, by metal tongues speaking in open peals of joy or in muffled accents of death, and by trainmen cheerily yanking a cord for the next stop.

The bell in its highest form is perhaps the carillon. Carillons were defined by the Carillon Guild in its Sixth Congress in 1946 as: "An instrument comprising at least two octaves of fixed cup-shaped bells arranged in chromatic series and so tuned as to produce, when many such bells are sounded together, concordant harmony. It is normally played from a keyboard which controls expression through variation of touch."

In a sort of Christmas pilgrimage I once went to the Riverside Church singing tower with its seventy-two bells in six chromatic octaves. Arriving before the appointed time for my interview with Kamiel Lefévere, the carillonneur, I made use of the extra minutes to climb the five or so flights of iron-work stairs (I had already been shunted up twenty stories by elevator) to the wide tower with the bells hung at intervals and the stairs winding about. The world's largest tuned bell is there, 40,926 pounds of it. It is *big!* I could have fitted a bed, a dresser, several chairs, and a table snugly under the bell's copious spread.

I paced around it. At the quarter hour the bells began to play. Then came the great B-O-N-G, B-O-N-G of this large bell. (Its clapper alone weighs a half ton!) As I fled up another flight of stairs, the sound pursued me like swift wind. For minutes afterward I heard its hum, and it was to linger in my ears for days. From the top of the tower I looked down through the stonework at the tiny figures below. That woman in the scarlet coat, that infinitesimal child running, that tiny row of bench sitters— the great bell sounded for them and for thousands of others to hear.

I searched out Dr. Lefévere at the carillon's console, in a glass-incased room in the midst of the bells. The console is very much like an organ keyboard. The "keys," however, are round, smooth, and protruding, like small broom sticks. Sharps and flats are arranged as on the piano, above and between the "white" keys. The foot pedals are similarly placed, are heavier than organ pedals, and are covered with rubber or leather. These pedals set the heavier bells to ringing. Since the keys are thumped with the *bent* little finger, it is the custom among carillonneurs to wear heavy leather gloves cut away to leave the fingers free, but incasing the lower part of the hand.

Another difficulty the carillonneur has to face is that there is no music written directly for carillon. (This is because each carillon is different from every other.) Each carillonneur thus becomes his own arranger, and, at times, his own composer. Dr. Lefévere told me of the interest he took in arranging Christmas carols for broadcast to Europe during the World War II, at the request of the Office of

War Information, first going to Greek restaurants and French pastry shops and Italian fruit stores to get at the songs at their source.

The carillon takes real strength to manipulate. That I believed when Dr. Lefévere sat down at the console and began what can only be called his gymnastics. He can hardly be compared with the church organist, sedate and immaculate. He tears over the keyboard, thumping vigorously with fisted hands. His arms fling out to the right and to the left; his feet cavort in a strange dance. At the close of so simple a tune as Brahms's Waltz in A, he is ringing wet with perspiration. After such a presentation, it is easy to understand why so few women have entered the field of carillon playing.

It isn't as though he were playing by remote control, however. For there is the lever pulling down the string that controls the clapper.* Since the clapper is only a fraction of an inch from the bell's edge, it responds to this pull immediately. You play and the bell sounds. The contact is as personal as the plucking of a harp string.

Dr. Lefévere has spent practically his whole life playing on bells here and in Belgium, and it is his ambition to arouse civic consciousness to the need of carillons in small towns throughout the land. "No town should be without at least a modest set," he explains earnestly. "It is a force for democracy." When the bells were taken by the Nazis from European belfries to melt down for guns, the towns'

---

* Three sorts of clappers are fixed within the larger bells, one to use when the console is played, one to use when the drum with pegs (like a player piano roll) chimes the hours, and one to use when the bells are swung.

inhabitants could not rest until they were restored. Little wonder, when every event in the community is pointed up by bells. Civic-owned bells, Dr. Lefévere contends, sound for all alike—both sides of the railroad track, all peoples, all races.

Particularly appropriate are they for the underlining of events that reach all humankind alike. Thus Dr. Lefévere played the carillon when four trees were planted in a park in upper Manhattan in memory of those four chaplains of different faiths, in World War II, who stood hand in hand on a sinking ship that those in their spiritual charge might live. Thus bells greeted the homecoming of our heroes after the war. And thus a bell was used to bring the idea of freedom, international and inter-racial, before the whole world.

But he emphasizes if we are to have bells in our small towns they should be *tuned* bells, not the kind that hang in so many church towers in our country and make the onward Christian soldier stumble in his tracks, and the kindly light lead ever so falteringly. He was very explicit about the tuning. A bell differs from, say, a violin or wind instrument in that its partials, like the rainbow's colors, are not entirely absorbed in the whole. A bell is divided into several parts according to the rate of vibration:

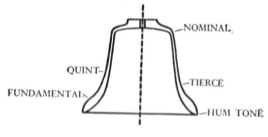

The clapper strikes where "fundamental" is indicated. But the other portions, vibrating, either conflict with (as in untuned bells) or amplify (as in tuned bells) the sound. A carillon bell has been tuned to incredible accuracy and purity; tuned, moreover, in such a way that it is incapable ever again of getting out of tune.

Bell tuning is an art in itself. "A perfectly cast bell, one that needs no tuning," says Mrs. A. S. C. Forbes of Los Angeles, one of our country's few women bell-founders, "is rare and priceless as a Stradivarius." A bell to be pleasant to the ears has to be tuned. Tuning is accomplished by paring off ever so carefully certain portions of the metal—copper and tin are used for bells—while the inverted bell is being rotated below a cutting tool. When a bell is properly tuned, there are definite and unvarying intervals between the partials:

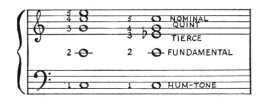

A "peal" of bells is a group of such bells fashioned to ring together—each bell tuned not only with itself but with the other members of its group. In this country a peal usually consists of three bells, tuned to the first, third, and fifth tones of the musical scale. When four bells are used, the eighth musical tone is added. Probably most popular among chimes is the "Westminster peal" from an air commonly attributed to Handel:

The peal used by the Riverside Church in New York for marking the hours is that phrase from Wagner's *Parsifal*, sounding as Parsifal wanders through the flowered fields in search of the Holy Grail:

When this same phrase is sounded at the Metropolitan Opera performance, four metal sheets tuned to the proper tones and hit with a hammer are used. The piano supplies the requisite overtones.

The orchestra, as we have seen, also uses bells: the glockenspiel, celesta, tubular chimes, gong, triangle, and even sleigh bells. With this battery, composers can express church bells, elfin bells, temple music, and any of the other tintinnabulations emitted by struck metal.

Debussy, whose sonorities "seem to merge and dissolve in iridescent mists," was an interested listener to Javanese music (almost all bells) when it was played at the Paris Exposition. He experimented endlessly with chord combinations to make them sound like bells he had heard in his childhood. He thought of a chord not as one gesture leading into another in a sort of endless dance (the usual Western concept) but as a tone-posture complete and apart—a thing of beauty in itself. In short, the bell concept. Thus the "sonorous halo" which surrounds his works.

But back to bells as they sound in the open air. There's the electric carillon which has certain points in its favor. It's comparatively cheap; it's comparatively portable; and it's comparatively easy to manipulate. When the keys are pressed, the tiny hammers strike small metal reeds which sound the notes—five or so octaves—in a carillon scale. These notes, electrically amplified, are sent out far and wide through a loudspeaker system located in the bell-less tower. Soft and loud effects are obtained by pressing the key lightly or heavily. A special foot "swell" allows for some excellent "tolling" effects.

While electric carillons are in certain cases a necessity in this age of compression both in time and space, it is doubtful whether electricity can ever take over the role of bells in their symbolic field. The Freedom Bell could scarcely have had as pinch hitter an electrical vibration. For that Freedom Bell—like our Liberty Bell, which, though cracked, emits a more eloquent message than any bell-less church tower—is powerful through its very symbolism. Carved on it, according to the inspired design of Walter Dorwin Teague, are five figures representing the five major races of mankind, with arms outstretched, their hands joined by flaming torches, symbolic of truth. And speaking, even in the bell's silence, is its inscription, "That this world under God shall have a new birth of freedom."

# INDEX

# INDEX

# INDEX